A
Female Predator

When Women Stalk, Attack, Kill, Harass and Sexually Assault Other Women

Written by:

J. M. Gordon

Revised Edition

ACKNOWLEDGEMENTS

I'd like to thank author David Brakke, the late author M. Scott Peck M.D. and the late Father Malachi Martin for their fearless and incomparable works.

And

To forensic psychiatrist Dr. Michael Stone for his tireless efforts and ground breaking research in quantifying Evil.

To Leif, the man who will survive Ragnarok, my Guardian Angel. Thank You.

To my Beloved S.Z. Thank you for making me feel safe and sound.

To all those who shine light in dark places…Lux Perpetua.

A Female Predator

CONTENTS

8   Case Studies:

Women Who Kill Children

FORWARD

A Treatise on Evil

"If you lie, you'll steal, if you steal, you'll kill."

It is said that the full extent of evil cannot be quantified. To quantify evil would be a test in futility because evil can be most banal. Where it is not banal, it can be quite ferocious in its methodology, intent and delivery.

There are those who believe evil is merely a symptom of a neurological or emotional injury, illness or malfunction. I believe evil is also spiritual and karmic in nature to the extent which we will attempt to investigate and explain. It is my firm belief that many women are suffering from what I would call "Acute Gender Biased Jealousy Disorder".

Drawing a correlation between the psycho-social, neurological, medical-emotional and the para-psycological, one can begin to form a theory, to make sense of the inhumane and the depraved psyche of a predator.

People have tried to research what causes Evil, using time honored traditions, superstitions, spiritual and karmic guidelines but at times, I have found it easier to take a scientific approach. While taking a scientific approach I have found no other better research tool than that of forensic psychiatrist Dr. Michael Stone and the scale he created that quantifies evil.

The Most Evil Scale ranges from 1 through 22 categories. Category number 1 begins with those who kill in self defense, through category number 22 ending in serial torturer murderers. An individual's personal history, morality, ethics or lack thereof and pre-meditated motives are considered when placing an individual on the scale of evil. Using the scale, we will attempt to categorize and properly identify the female predator.

The main objective of this book is to explore the psycho social, neurological and or medical emotional reasons, or other hypothesis for female same sex violence, aggravated sexual assaults and murders. During the course of this book, we will explore Psychological Profiles and Case Studies of real non fictional crimes. At the end of the book there is also a Self Assessment and Help Guide for Survivors and Abusers who wish to learn more or find help.

Some of you may be reading this book and may have yourselves, committed an predatory act against another and perhaps you may have forgotten about it or it was never reported. This book is for both the abusers and for the abused. I hope it gives voice to the victims and helps anyone either struggling with or in some way suffering from these behaviors, to find help and healing.

STATISTICS

Rape and child abuse by women is vastly underreported. In society, we've created a sort of "Bitch Culture" that we're all familiar with, "the mean girl", "the femme fatal", the "tiger mom" and the super aggressive girlfriend are just some of the stereotypes that have been created to describe women who engage in very real and often unreported attacks against other women.

According to 1996 Health Canada Report As recently as 10 years ago, it was a common assumption that females did not or could not sexually abuse children or youth. Even some professionals working in the field believed that women represented only about 1% to 3% of sexual abusers at most. However, mounting research evidence about sexual abuse perpetration at the hands of teen and adult females has begun to challenge our assumptions, though these earlier and dated views still tend to predominate.

The percentage of women and teenage girl perpetrators recorded in case report studies is small and ranges from 3% to 10% (Kendall-Tackett and Simon, 1987; McCarty, 1986; Schultz and Jones, 1983; Wasserman and Kappel, 1985). When the victim is male, female perpetrators account for 1 % to 24% of abusers. When the victim is female, female perpetrators account for 6% to 17% of abusers (American Humane Association, 1981; Finkelhor and Russell, 1984; Finkelhor et al., 1990). In the Ontario Incidence Study, 10% of sexual abuse investigations involved female perpetrators (Trocme, 1994). However, in six studies reviewed by Russell and Finkelhor, female perpetrators accounted for 25% or more of abusers. Ramsay-Klawsnik (1990) found that adult females were abusers of males 37% of the time and female adolescents 19% of the time. Both of these rates are higher than the same study reported for adult and teen male abusers.

Some research has reported that female perpetrators commit fewer and less intrusive acts of sexual abuse compared to males. While male perpetrators are more likely to engage in anal intercourse and to have the victim engage in oral-genital contact, females tend to use more foreign objects as part of the abusive act (Kaufman et al., 1995).

This study also reported that differences were not found in the-frequency of vaginal intercourse, fondling by the victim or abuser, genital body contact without penetration or oral contact by the abuser.

Females may be more likely to use verbal coercion than physical force.

The most commonly reported types of abuse by female perpetrators include vaginal intercourse, oral sex, fondling and group sex (Faller, 1987; Hunter et al., 1993). However, women also engage in mutual masturbation, oral, anal and genital sex acts, show children pornography and play sex games (Johnson, 1989; Knopp and Lackey, 1987).

The research suggests that, overall, female and male perpetrators commit many of the same acts and follow many of the same patterns of abuse against their victims. They also do not tend to differ significantly in terms of their relationship to the victim (most are relatives) or the location of the abuse (Allen, 1990; Kaufman et al., 1995).

It is interesting to note in the study by Kaufman et al. (1995) that 8% of the female perpetrators were teachers and 23% were babysitters, compared to male perpetrators who were 0% and 8% respectively. Finkelhor et al. (1988) also report significantly higher rates of sexual abuse of children by females in day-care settings. Of course, Finkelhor's findings should not surprise us given that women represent the majority of day-care employees.

Research on teen and adult female sexual abuse perpetrators has found that many suffer from low self-esteem, antisocial behaviour, poor social and anger management skills, fear of rejection, passivity, promiscuity, mental health problems, post-traumatic stress disorder and mood disorders (Hunter et al., 1993; Mathews, Matthews and Speltz, 1989). However, as in the case of male perpetrators, research does not substantiate that highly emotionally disturbed or psychotic individuals predominate among the larger population of female sexual abusers (Faller, 1987).

There is some evidence that females are more likely to be involved with co-abusers, typically a male, though studies report a range from 25% to 77% (Faller, 1987; Kaufman et al., 1995; McCarty, 1986). However, Mayer (1992), in a review of data on 17 adolescent female sex offenders, found that only 2 were involved with male co-perpetrators. She also found that the young women in this study knew their victims and that none experienced legal consequences for their actions.

Self-report studies provide a very different view of sexual abuse perpetration and substantially increase the number of female perpetrators. In a retrospective study of male victims, 60% reported being abused by females (Johnson and Shrier, 1987). The same rate was found in a sample of college students (Fritz et al., l 981). In other studies of male university and college students, rates of female perpetration were found at levels as high as 72% to 82% (Fromuth and Burkhart, 1987, 1989; Seidner and Calhoun, 1984). Bell et al. (1981) found that 27% of males were abused by females. In some of these types of studies, females represent as much as 50% of sexual abusers (Risin and Koss, 1987).

Knopp and Lackey (1987) found that 51% of victims of female sexual abusers were male. It is evident that case report and self-report studies yield very different types of data about prevalence. These extraordinary differences tell us we need to start questioning all of our assumptions about perpetrators and victims of child maltreatment.

Finally, there is an alarmingly high rate of sexual abuse by females in the backgrounds of rapists, sex offenders and sexually aggressive men - 59% (Petrovich and Templer, 1984), 66%

(Groth, 1979) and 80% (Briere and Smiljanich, 1993). A strong case for the need to identify female perpetrators can be found in Table 4, which presents the findings from a study of adolescent sex offenders by O'Brien (1989).

Male adolescent sex offenders abused by "females only" chose female victims almost exclusively. The study also found that for men the perpetrators' victims tend to be either the same gender or female to be 67.5 %; while for female perpetrator's the victims tend to be 93.3% same sex.

In addition the Berkowitz (1993), in a Winnipeg-based study of sexually abused males in treatment groups, found interfamilial abuse at 72.2% in women vs. 100% in men, extrafamilial abuse at 54.5% in female adults, 43.6% for female adolescents vs. 90.9% male adults and 70.9% male adolescents.

According to a story entitled "Not only Men are Molesters" reported on August 16, 2002 by staff writer for The Los Angeles Times, Maura Dolan writes, "Women are less likely than men to commit sex offenses, but they also are less likely to be reported and prosecuted. Many experts contend that women commit sex offenses far more often than is generally believed."

"It happens a lot more than gets reported, and I think part of that is due to our culture," said Steven B. Blum, a consulting psychologist to a sex offender program in Nebraska. "There are a lot of women who have sexual contact with teenage boys, and they don't get reported."

Paul Federoff, a forensic psychiatrist in Ottawa, Canada, said one of the female sex offenders he counsels is an exhibitionist. She opens her living room curtains and strips off her clothes when people pass by.

He told her that unless she stopped this illegal activity, she would be arrested.

" 'Doctor, if someone calls up and says he saw me disrobing in the window, who do you think they are going to arrest? Me or him?' " Federoff said she replied.

"And she is absolutely right."

There are 351 men in California locked up in a state mental hospital as sexually violent predators, prone to attack again and again.

Then there is Charlotte Mae Thrailkill.

The 43-year-old mother of two is California's only female violent sex offender, confined to a maximum-security state mental hospital after experts decided she was too dangerous for release.

Only a handful of women, including Thrailkill, have ever been confined to mental institutions under state laws that allow for civil commitments of sex criminals after they have served their prison terms.

It was widely assumed until recently that women just didn't sexually abuse children, Federoff said.

But during the past two decades, as parents and others have encouraged children to disclose improper sexual behavior, kids have been confiding about abuse by women as well as men.

"Now we are discovering that there are a lot of women who do sexually abuse children, but they get away with it," Federoff said. "There is a growth industry of treatment programs, particularly for adolescent female sex offenders who commit a lot of the crimes while they are baby-sitting."

Thrailkill, whose sexual predator status is up for review by the state, told psychiatrists she molested children, ages 5 to 8, whom she baby-sat or enticed into her Santa Rosa apartment to play with her children. Her story, pieced together from court records, is a less a rarity than crime statistics suggest.

Thrailkill, the third of six children, was born with scoliosis and a deformity in her mouth that caused speech difficulties. "She stated that school was difficult for her, not only due to her learning difficulties but also due to constant ridicule by her peers because of her physical deformities," according to a state mental heath report on file in Santa Rosa.

When older children picked on her during elementary school, "she would then bully and beat smaller, defenseless children," according to the May 2000 report.

She told counselors that she had a good relationship with her father, but complained that her mother regularly beat her with narrow leather straps, sticks and her fists. Thrailkill ran away several times between the ages of 11 and 16 and was gang-raped at age 15, she told authorities, by four men who grabbed her off a street.

That same year she was severely wounded in a random shooting and spent nine months in a hospital. She never returned to school.

Thrailkill married a U.S. Marine at 19. They had two daughters. She left him five years later, complaining their marriage was sexless, and won custody of their daughters.

Women who commit sex offenses often fit into one of three categories.

The "teacher-lover" or "Mrs. Robinson" type has sex with underage boys. These women fancy themselves in love with the boy and don't see the relationships as harmful, experts say.

The women tend to be immature and get an "ego boost" from the involvement, said Blum, the Nebraska psychologist, who counsels such offenders. "Without exception, all of our patients have had a substance abuse problem and also were partying with their victims," he said.

"Generally the male doesn't feel victimized," he said. "A lot of teenage boys would see that as their lucky day."

Despite such perceptions, researchers maintain that many boys may be left confused and angry, and if they are particularly young, they may be sexualized too early and have sexual problems later in life.

Women who have sex with minors make the same kinds of excuses as their male counterparts, said Florence Wolfe, co-director of Northwest Treatment

Associates, a Seattle-based program for sex offenders.

Wolfe said the women tell her: " 'I wanted the closeness, the excitement, not the sex. I wanted the safety. He was 13. I was only 27. The kid wanted it.' "

A study of college students and prisoners found that 16% of the college men and 46% of the male prisoners reported they had sexual experience before the age of 16 with a woman at least five years older. The average age of the men at the time of the contact was 12.

A second type of offender is called "predisposed" and includes mothers who molest their children.

Wolfe says more than 50% of the 150 female offenders she has counseled molested their own children, primarily daughters.

Some women considered predisposed to sexually molest children are pedophiles with an assortment of mental illnesses. Wolfe described one such offender she has met as a sexual sadist.

"She looks like everybody's lovable grandmother: pink cheeks, gray hair, chunky," Wolfe said. "She volunteered to baby-sit for young single moms. They jumped at the chance."

Most of this offender's victims were girls, and most were not yet verbal. The woman would slap them until their teeth cut their mouths or start a nosebleed. Their pain gave her sexual pleasure, Wolfe said.

"She finally molested a 4-year-old, and that kid was verbal enough to tell someone," Wolfe said.

The third type of female sex criminal is called the "male-coerced" or "male-accompanied" offender. These women commit sex crimes in the company of a man. Thrailkill, who declined to be interviewed fits in this category.

Thrailkill told psychologists that she had sex with 20 to 50 different men in the year after her divorce. She eventually met Daryl Ball and allowed him and his young sons to move into her apartment in Santa Rosa. Ball introduced Thrailkill to sex with children, according to a state Mental Health Department report filed with Santa Rosa Superior Court.

Thrailkill at the time was thin, with long, dark blond hair. She looked older than her 27 years. She was quiet, shy and submissive, attorneys recall.

Seven years her senior, Ball was a brutal boyfriend, Thrailkill told others. She said he violently sodomized her, threw her from a car once and beat her to unconsciousness twice.

She molested his sons, police said. Not only was Ball aware of the molestations, he joined her in having sex with children, police and criminal records say.

Ball and Thrailkill had sex a couple of times a day with children and with as many as five children at a time, she told psychiatrists. The victims were her boyfriend's sons and other children in the apartment complex whom Thrailkill baby-sat or lured into their apartment.

During the eight months in which she molested, Thrailkill drank and used methamphetamine, first snorting the drug and later injecting it, she told mental health workers.

"When she was intoxicated, she was sexually promiscuous, violent and sexually perverse," according to a May 2001 report by the state Department of Mental Health.

Both Thrailkill and Ball threatened the children that their parents or siblings would be killed if they told anyone. Eventually, one of the children did tell, and Thrailkill and Ball were arrested.

When a parent of one of the victims confronted Thrailkill, she said she molested because she was "afraid" of Ball, who was then 34.

"He made me do it," she said.

But in records on file at the Santa Rosa courthouse, Thrailkill admitted she molested five children — four boys and one girl — on her own. She said she abused them to get even with the victims' parents.

Thrailkill typically endured extensive mistreatment in relationships, a mental health evaluation found. When she finally felt sufficiently hurt by the abuse, she lashed out at others.

"She admits she takes anger out on weaker, often innocent individuals," a mental health counselor wrote.

A 1981 national study of both reported and unreported child abuse indicated that as many as 24% of boys and 14% of girls who are molested are victimized by women.

Although sexual abuse by both men and women is underreported, female offenders are less likely than men to be prosecuted.

"I have had so many clients, both males and females, who talked about mothers or their baby-sitters molesting them," said Charlene Steen, a psychologist in Napa who has treated sex offenders for 20 years. "And they were never reported."

Dr. Robert Kolodny, who has directed behavioral research institutes and written about sexual behavior, said he periodically gets calls from befuddled prosecutors who have cases in which a man has accused a woman of rape.

"Although it sounds counterintuitive, men can indeed be raped," Kolodny said.

People commonly assume that men cannot be forced into sex against their will. But experts say men may be physically capable of sex even while under extreme duress.

Female rapists are sometimes acquaintances of their victims and get them drunk or drugged before they force them to submit to sexual acts.

"We don't really have good studies that would give us an accurate picture of how often it happens, but it is not rare ... not a one-in-a-thousand kind of thing," Kolodny said.

Some case studies describe rapes of men committed by two or more women. In a report in the Archives of Sexual Behavior, two physicians described 11 cases of rapes of men, including a man who picked up a woman in a bar and then went to a motel with her.

The man had a drink and fell asleep, the 1982 report said. When he awoke, he was gagged, blindfolded and tied to the bed. He heard the voices of several women.

Steen, who is also a lawyer, described one man who was drugged and raped by two women and a man. The victim was later found wandering the streets with his clothes tied around his neck.

Observed Steen: "There are women out there who are doing some pretty horrible things."

Thrailkill initially faced more than 50 counts of felony child molesting. She pleaded no contest in 1988 to five counts of molestation in exchange for a 14-year prison sentence.

Ball, whom Thrailkill married after the arrests but divorced while in prison, pleaded no contest to several counts of lewd and lascivious conduct upon children and was sentenced to 24 years in prison.

Thrailkill began serving her sentence in September 1988 and was paroled in September 1994. She then worked in construction and had what court records described as two "normal" relationships with adult men.

In July 1996, she violated her parole by using alcohol, associating with convicted sex offenders and having contact with children.

She returned to prison and again was paroled in March 1998. Within a month, parole was revoked because she had used alcohol. The state began proceedings to commit her as a sex predator, and she did not oppose the effort.

Marie Case, a Santa Rosa criminal defense lawyer who represented her, said Thrailkill was "intimidated by the whole proceeding" and horrified that media coverage might hurt her daughters, who were then in school.

"I found her to be very shy and very private, and it was very painful for her to discuss" her past, Case said.

Thrailkill was certified as a sexually violent predator in September 1998 and sent to Patton State Hospital in San Bernardino County.

Like other sex predators who have been committed, Thrailkill's status must be reviewed by the state every two years. She may be recommitted only if two mental health experts determine her mental problems make her likely to molest again.

During therapy, she has expressed regret about her two daughters, who are now adults. Thrailkill conceded at the hospital that her daughters had been "sexual victims of her husband

and emotional victims of her," a report said.

Ball, now 50, was released on parole. Two state-appointed mental health experts evaluated him and found he does not have a mental disorder that makes him likely to molest again.

Thrailkill is scheduled to leave Patton in September unless the state tries to renew her commitment.

A staff psychologist with the department wrote that Thrailkill does not wish to be released until she is convinced she can "manage" her behavior. According to a May 2000 report, she has "genuine shame for her behavior and remorse for her victims."

"She has never shown any interest in coming out," Case said. "I think she feels safe there."

Unfortunately there are many examples of female predators at their terrible work. Another story, as reported in the Edmonton Journal Jan 29th 2010 by Sarah Sacheli entitled "Female sexual abusers not as rare as widely believed" details the story of a mother who made pornographic images of her two year old son. Sarah Sacheli writes, "She gave him life and was the only parent he ever knew. In the way she snapped photos of him sleeping and playing happily, she was like any other adoring mother. But she also committed unspeakable acts to his little body, turning him into a human sex toy in her pornographic broadcasts.

The set of facts involving the Windsor-area mother who sexually abused her two-year-old son horrified both those involved in the case and those who'd only heard about it.

"Society expects the mother of a toddler would do everything in her power to make sure her child is protected from harm," said the judge who handed the

24-year-old woman a 3 1/2-year prison sentence.

He called her crimes "appalling" and "abhorrent."

While female sexual abusers are rare in the court system, those who deal with child sexual abuse know the woman is not unique. She may be the first Ontario woman to be jailed for making child pornography featuring her own offspring, but she's not the first mother to sexually abuse a child.

A national study released in 2005 shows that biological mothers were the perpetrators of sexual abuse in 5% of the substantiated cases investigated by child welfare authorities.

The instance is probably higher, since researchers are certain that many cases of child sexual abuse never come to light. "A lot of people have difficulty believing women are capable of sexually abusing children," said social worker Angela Hovey, whose doctoral thesis deals with a topic related to this theme.

Even victims of such abuse, looking back at it as adults, have a hard time talking about it.

In her past employment in federal prisons, she would ask inmates about any sexual abuse in their past. "Many men had been abused by women." The problem, she said, was "they often had more difficulty identifying it as abuse."

A U.S. report, entitled "Child Sexual Abuse -- The Predators," explains it this way. "Mothers generally have more intimate contact with their children, and the lines between maternal love and care and sexual abuse are not as clear-cut as they are for fathers."

Therefore, the report says, "Sexual abuse by mothers may remain undetected because it occurs at home and is either denied or never reported."

Hovey says it's hard to get accurate data on the prevalence of female sex offenders, much less women who abuse their own children. The best information, she believes, may come from victims themselves.

A 2003 U.S. study questioned a random sample of adults to determine the prevalence of childhood sexual abuse. It found that of the 32% of females and 14% of males who identified themselves as victims, 9% of women and 39% of men said they had been abused by at least one female.

While figures are usually inflated, studies of male sex offenders show 45% to 50% were themselves victims of sexual abuse. Hovey is researching counseling practices for women survivors of sexual abuse to see if they should be asked if they've ever in turn abused anyone. She saw it in her private practice -- women sexually abusing children.

"Do I think it happens a lot more than we hear about? Absolutely," said Bill Bevan, executive director of the Windsor-Essex Children's Aid Society -- which sees two or three such cases each year.

Most don't end up in prosecutions because the young victims aren't capable of testifying. "It could be a teacher. It could be a sister. It could be a babysitter. It could be a mother with her child."

Society jokes that teenage boys abused by women are somehow "lucky" and females, by nature, are too nurturing to commit such an offence. In any case of child sexual abuse, there's "kind of gender bias" that automatically excludes women from suspicion, Bevan said.

"It's not the first place you look. It's the father figure you look at first."

Canadians think of female sex offenders, and their minds automatically turn to Karla Homolka who, with her then husband, Paul Bernardo, abducted, sexually abused, tortured and murdered female victims, Bevan said.

"On the other end of the scale is where the female in the caring role takes in a partner who is abusing the child.... Some mothers might be kind of looking the other way."

Justice Kathryn Feldman, in a Jan. 18 Ontario Court of Appeal case, said the Internet is providing greater opportunity to produce and distribute images of child abuse.

"The victims are innocent children who become props in a perverted show, played out for an ever-wider audience not only of voyeurs but of perpetrators," Feldman said of a case involving a father who sexually abused his daughter and distributed the images over the Internet.

"The predominant offender in Internet child exploitation is males," said Windsor police Det. Jason Belanger. "They're out there, but if you do get a female offender, you're surprised."

In the United Kingdom of Liverpool, a 29 year old tennis coach was found by her 13 year old victims mother in bed performing sex acts with one another. As reported to the Daily Mail by writer James Tozer on Oct 3rd 2007, "The mother of a young tennis star yesterday described the moment she allegedly found the 13-year-old and her female coach naked in bed together.

The woman said she screamed "You are nothing but a pedophile!" at 29-year-old Claire Lyte after stumbling across the pair performing sex acts on each other.

However, she told a court she did not report the incident to police because Lyte's father begged her not to ruin her coaching career and insisted it would not happen again.

It was not until nearly a year later that she became convinced the illicit lesbian relationship had continued and informed the authorities, she said.

When she found out that police were involved, her daughter climbed onto the roof of their house and threatened to commit suicide, she added, although she was later talked down.

The girl, who cannot be identified legal reasons, initially told police the bedroom incident had been a one-off, but she now claims this was a lie and that Lyte had threatened to destroy her tennis career if she exposed the alleged abuse.

Her mother was giving evidence at Liverpool Crown Court where Lyte – who until injury ended her career was one of Britain's top women players - is accused of sexual activity with a child.

The coach denies the charges, saying the 'pushy and ambitious' mother concocted the allegations after her daughter's tennis career stalled.

The girl's mother dabbed at tears as she described the incident in October 2005 when she came home unexpectedly and allegedly found them in bed together.

"My daughter jumped up and ran off and Claire pulled the bed sheet over her head," she said.

"Claire stayed in the bed under the sheet, and I shouted at both of them to get some clothes on and come downstairs.

 "I was screaming at Claire, "Get out, what have you done, what have you done to my child, you are nothing but a pedophile".

"They came downstairs dressed, and my daughter sat down in a chair and curled into a ball. Claire sat with her head in her hands.

"Claire just kept telling me she loved my daughter. I kept saying, "She is 13". My daughter just cried and cried."

She said after talking for hours, Lyte agreed to cease coaching her daughter and distance herself from her.

The next day the mother took her daughter back to the prestigious Lawn Tennis Association academy in Loughborough which she attended.

Later that day, however, she said Lyte's father Colin rang 'begging' to meet her.

She eventually relented, driving to a motorway cafe that evening to discuss what had happened.

She told the court: "Colin pleaded with me not to do anything, to let him sort it out.

"He said he couldn't let her career end like this. He said he would really sort Claire out and this would never happen again."

But two weeks later, when the mother demanded to look at a text message on her daughter's phone, the girl locked herself in the toilet and threatened to ring ChildLine because her mother was 'abusing' her.

"I was so upset and furious and felt it was all connected with Claire," she said.

Lyte had meanwhile been warned by bosses at the academy for becoming too close to girl players and had been found sharing a toilet cubicle with the 13-year-old, the court heard.

Her mother said she reluctantly accepted Mr Lyte's assurances but in

August last year she saw them getting out of a minibus together and realized Lyte was wearing her daughter's clothes, she said.

"I knew then I had to go to the police," she said.

When police raided Lyte's home they found clothing allegedly belonging to the girl.

These included a pair of pink knickers with her name tag sewn into them which were shown to the jury.

Lyte, from Shirley, near Solihull, West Midlands, denies five counts of sexual activity with a child between May 2005 and June last year. Lyte was jailed for nearly three years for the conviction.

A story for the website "The Conservative Voice" as reported by writer Gordon Finley (Professor of Psychology at Florida International University in Miami Florida, U.S.A.)

August 08, 2006 states, "From the increasing frequency with which reports of female teachers having sex with their pupils are appearing in the print and electronic media to Lauren Books' article My Nanny Molested Me in an issue of Seventeen magazine, concerned citizens have every right to be asking themselves: What is going on here? And, perhaps most critically: Is this the tip of the iceberg?"

"Basically, the answer is yes, it is the tip of the iceberg. It also is fair to ask: How do we know? It is difficult to know with precision because female sexual predators have been a politically incorrect topic and thus hidden from public view.

However, we do know that the few professionals who have worked in the area universally acknowledge massive underreporting by the boy and girl victims of female sexual predators and, even when reports of female sexual molestation emerge, they are met with disbelief by parents and police."

"Critically, we now have sufficient preliminary research evidence and well documented case reports to know that we do have a serious social problem which requires immediate public, Congressional, and Judicial attention. Consider first the research."

"A 2004 U. S. Department of Education report titled Educator Sexual Misconduct: A Synthesis of Existing Literature cites two large sample surveys in which students report that 43% of their molesters were female sexual predators while smaller studies reported lower rates.

This second group estimates that 25% of sexual predators are female but also cite studies where the female predator rates range from 1% to 82% with six studies reporting female predator rates over 50%."

"Taken together, these research studies substantiate the reality that we currently are experiencing an epidemic of female sexual predators. These reported rates are high by any standard and require immediate attention and corrective action."

"The most emotionally traumatic and moving evidence, however, comes not from statistical studies but from heart rending individual case reports.

The best of this evidence can be found in a groundbreaking documentary aired by the British Broadcasting Corporation on October 6, 1997, titled The Ultimate Taboo: Child Sexual abuse by women. This was a vivid and horrific program in which the victims of sexual abuse by women told disturbing stories of emotional and physical damage."

"As the evidence continues to mount -- the daily media reports, the BBC documentary, the empirical research studies -- it becomes increasingly clear that the veiled epidemic of female sexual predators no longer can be hidden and must be brought to full public light and serve as a call for social change.

As a society we require a massive change in our social attitudes to begin to address the fact that the people to whom we have most entrusted our children for centuries -- mothers, babysitters, nuns, nannies, child care workers, and teachers include female sexual predators."

"In my view, Child Abuse Prevention Month -- April 2006 -- provides a unique opportunity to face squarely the politically incorrect reality that female sexual predators do exist, do prey, and do so in substantial numbers. It also provides an opportunity to create a paradigm shift wherein we reframe the sexual abuse debate and acknowledge the existence of both male and female sexual predators."

"Continuing to deny that female sexual predators exist, prey, and do so in substantial numbers not only continues to endanger our children but also damages them -- physically, emotionally, and in their subsequent relationships with others."

"Denial serves only the best interests of practicing female sexual predators and those who keep their secrets."

PSYCHOLOGICAL PROFILES

EARLY CHILDHOOD
Fact Vs. Myth

In learning to understand the mind of a sex offender, the first step is to learn to separate facts from myths. In this chapter, we will explore some of the most common myths concerning sex offenders and we will summarize what research has shown concerning these issues. Although the study of female sex offenders is a relatively new field and research is constantly being updated, we will attempt to explore its depths.

J. M. Gordon

Myth: Only males commit sex offenses.

Fact: Both male and females commit sex offenses

Don't believe it, here are some statistics:

Of the 12,992 people whose cases were disposed of between 2005 and 2006 for sexual offenses in New York State, 97% were male (New York State Sex Offender Management Grant, 2007). Therefore, we estimate that 3% were female.

(That's roughly 390 Female Sex Offenders)

As of December 2007, about 2% of the people required to register under New York's Sex Offender Registration Act (SORA) were female (data from the New York State Division of Criminal Justice Services, Sex Offender Registry).

(That's roughly 510 Female Sex Offenders)

The New York data are similar to those reported in other states. For example, in 12 states between 1991 and 1996, 96% of the individuals in sexual assaults reported to law enforcement were male. From that we can calculate that 4% were female. **It is interesting that females were charged with a higher percentage of assaults against victims under age six.**

Myth: Children who are sexually assaulted will grow up to sexually assault others.

Fact: A Significant percentage of sex offenders were indeed abused as children although certainly not the majority.

Becker and Murphy (1998) estimated that while 30% of sex offenders were sexually abused as children, 70% were not.

Hindman and Peters (2001) found that 67% of sex offenders initially reported experiencing sexual abuse as children, but when given a polygraph ("lie detector") test, the proportion dropped to 29%, suggesting that some sex offenders exaggerate early childhood victimization in an effort to rationalize their behavior or gain sympathy from others.

So, what is the psychological profile of a female sexual predator and how is it different from that of her male counterpart? A female sexual predator is a deviant and from pre adolescence begins to express a pattern of deviant behaviors as she goes along. As she matures, the behaviors can be observed as either subtle, passive aggressive, aggravated or violent in nature. Each ones path to sexually predatory behavior varies. However, each predatory behavior can be said to share a common beginning: early childhood.

Some examples are :

Dominant Personality in which the child is always very demanding; singling out one or a few "weaker" children to focus on.

Aggressively plays with others in a very coercive and dominant way. Is usually ill responsive to the complaints of the "weaker" children or is Apathetic.

Obsessively concerned with her appearance or the appearance of other children.

Displays a masculine dominant and aggressive personality.

Demonstrates pathological lying and understands from a very early age how to do so as well as the benefits of doing so.

Hides articles or averts blame or withholds information.

Is coercive and ignores the will of others. It is a Myth to think that children fail to understand even from an early age, how to groom. They may not know what grooming is, however, the lack of self awareness doesn't prevent them from acting out even over a long period of time, the process of grooming.

From age 4 may start to outwardly demonstrate psychotic behavior. Psychotic behavior can seem like having a preternatural awareness of ways to aggravate and the child will be thrilled at doing so. Psychopaths can be frightening. A primitive term for Psychopathy is "Evil".

From as early as inside the womb a child learns to understand its environment. Children are thinkers! Just because they're pre verbal, doesn't mean they're little minds aren't ticking away. A child can begin to associate pain with pleasure months before they are able to verbalize.

A child can begin to understand the benefits of lying, hiding, or being the dominant personality, especially within a group. Just as adults are able to benefit from being dominant personalities children can also learn from predisposition how to behave. So one begs to ask the question, "What if anything, do I have to do with my child's abhorrent behavior?" Well, sociological research seems to point to genetics. A maleficent or degenerative gene, coupled with a child's environment and the socialization of his family have quite a bit to do with it. A child predisposed to an abusive same sex parent can have a latent homosexual urge to explore this type of homoerotic feeling but not necessarily to explore a homosexual relationship in and of itself. Its believed this is what leads to a separation inside the primary personality called the "Self", that creates another separate personality that is responsible for those feelings. Whether the person's Conscious mind has some sense of there being an "Other" in the background, needs to be further explored. Certainly when speaking of children, one could hypothesize that children are self aware to a degree but not a significant one as to make any pertinent changes to the self on their own.

Pedophilia

Category
Paraphilias and Sexual Disorders

Etiology
A large percentage of individuals with this disorder were sexually abused as children, although the vast majority of adults who were abused do *not* develop pedophilia or pedophilic behaviors. There is also those who argue pedophilia results from feelings of inadequacy with same age peers, and therefore a transfer of sexual urges to children.

Symptoms
This disorder is characterized by either intense sexually arousing fantasies, urges, or behaviors involving sexual activity with a prepubescent child (typically age 13 or younger). To be considered for this diagnosis, the individual must be at least 16 years old and at least 5 years older than the child.

Treatment

Treatment typically involves intensive psychotherapy to work on deep rooted issues concerning sexuality, feelings of self, and often childhood abuse. Medical treatments such as 'chemical castration' (which is actually a hormone medication which reduces testosterone and therefore sexual urges) have been investigated with very mixed results.

Pedophilia

Prognosis

Prognosis varies, although it is typically good if the individual has insight into his behaviors and his own childhood issues. Combined with an antisocial personality (which is usually what is seen on the news or in movies), however, treatment prognosis declines, sometimes significantly.

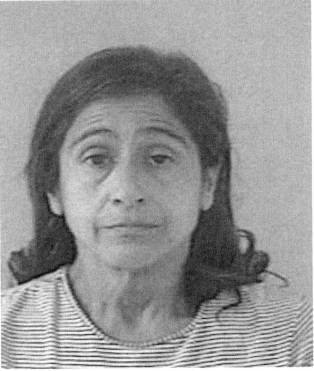

NANCY GARRIDO

PSYCHOLOGICAL PROFILE
ADOLECENCE
Fact Vs. Myth

Myth: Adolescents do not commit sex crimes.

Fact: Adolescents represent a fair number of sex offenders.

- Roughly 1,100 (8%) of arrests with dispositions in New York State between 2005 and 2006 for sexual offenses were committed by perpetrators under the age of 18 (New York State Sex Offender Management Grant, 2007).
- Nationally, 23% of sexual assault offenders were under the age of 18. About 4% were under the age of twelve. Forty percent of the offenders who assaulted children under the age of six were themselves less than 18 (Bureau of Justice Statistics, 2000).
- Approximately one-third of sexual offenses against children are committed by teenagers. Sexual offenses against young children under 12 years of age are typically committed by boys between the ages of 12 and 15 (Office of Juvenile Justice and Delinquency Prevention, 1999; Davis & Leitenberg, 1987).

During the adolescent stage a young female predator may begin to struggle with latent homoerotic feelings experienced during pre adolescence. This tends to lead to outwardly seeking behavior where the young predator begins to either openly but usually secretly experiment with these urges. Some outwardly seeking characteristics are:

- Intensely noticing other female infants, girls or women

- Obsessive feelings about other female infants, girls or women

- Bullying behavior either Individually or within a group while exhibiting Coercive Dominate behavior

- Exploiting trust either within the family or within a friendship

- Creates opportunities to isolate a perceived weaker individual in preparation for experimentation or grooming.

- Develops delusional and overly judgmental ideas about her female peers, may present jealousy

- Likes to create a sexually shameful environment for the perceived weaker victim, wherein the objectified person's physical person is either fondled or touched and while doing so is ridiculed

- May present bi-sexual feelings towards her female peers, which is passive aggressively explored though normal friendships or play

Myth: Most sexual offenses are committed by strangers.

Fact: Most sexual offenses are committed by family members or acquaintances.

In an article for The Forensic Panel entitled: "Sex grooming no science, but a technique: Lower standards admits testimony" by Jonathan Schiff Esq. reports on: *State of Oregon v. Bennett Stafford*

The prosecution had a problem with its case against a roving pedophile whose most recent gig occurred at a tutoring center. The child he was tutoring, and also grooming, caught on quickly to his real intentions when he began touching her thigh and chest, making her uncomfortable. Her complaint sparked an investigation, which turned up another little girl at the center so reporting his interest in her thighs and breasts. In this case, her resistance led to threats of harm if she told anybody.

An investigation ensued that led to criminal charges of attempted sex abuse and coercion.

The State's problem was to prove criminal intent since quick thinking by an intended victim had foreclosed any further opportunities for contact by the defendant. The State produced for its case several adult women who related being molested as children by the defendant many years earlier. The prosecution also relied heavily on the testimony of a clinical psychologist whose specialty was treating sex offenders. He testified about the seduction ritual known as grooming, the goal of which is the sexual victimization of a child.

The psychologist further testified in response to a hypothetical question, that the defendant's offending history, along with his recent behavior including his choice of occupation, interaction directed to relaxing the child's defenses and inappropriate escalating physical contact, established the grooming pattern.

Holding: The Court affirmed the conviction, dismissing the argument that the psychologist had testified to a scientific theory that was not established as valid through scientific testing and general acceptance among scientists. The Court held that the psychologist's opinion was not unlike the testimony of other professionals such as police officers and social workers. These experts are permitted to present opinions based on "technical and other specialized knowledge," which, considering the years of experience this witness had observing human behavior, was sufficient to establish its legitimacy.

The reasoning utilized by the court attempting to distinguish between scientific theory and expert knowledge was not, however, embraced by the majority. The majority agreed with the result, but several felt uncomfortable with a rule that would allow such exotic concepts as the grooming rituals of the American pedophile into evidence without first establishing the scientific validity of the concept.

Mr. Sinclair comments:

In the context of the sexual molestation of children, the term grooming may seem incongruous. Yet the closest familiar analog to grooming is the common ritual of courting.

How do child molesters groom potential victims? Like the man engaged in courting, the child molester behaves in ways to promote trust; and since the victim is often a part of a family, he will also try to gain the trust of the child's parents or care-providers. Child molesters often select their potential victims carefully, typically targeting the child who is seeking adult attention. Most often there is some period before the molester engages in any inappropriate behavior. During this time, the molester presents himself positively to the child, exhibits interest, is complimentary, and behaves in exemplary ways to reassure anyone who may be suspicious of his motives.

Once trust is accomplished, the child molester will begin to test and erode typical boundaries to sexual behavior. He might suggest that the child and he sleep in the same bed, be nude together, or he may touch the child near the genital area to test the child's reaction. He may suggest that the child engage in non-sexual inappropriate behaviors such as drinking alcohol, in order to make the child fearful that he or she will be in trouble if their activities together are discovered.

If the child does not appear overly upset or report these boundary violations to others, then the molester might escalate the intrusiveness of his sexual behaviors. Ultimately, the goal of grooming is to obtain compliance so the child will be available for sexual abuse.

For example, the child molester frequently will tell the child that touching between them is good, that it is an indication of their special relationship, and that if the child reports the behavior they will no longer be able to be friends. Some molesters threaten, and tell the child that by not complying with the touching the child, or some person important to the child, will be harmed.

If a man is interested in having sex with a woman, he knows success is unlikely if he simply approaches her and suggests sex. Instead, he will present his positive attributes and himself as someone interested in her. Often he will seek to gain the trust and approval of her friends and family. Frequently the courtship process is reciprocal, each actively courting the other.

Similarly, grooming behaviors employed by sex offenders are intended to increase the likelihood of success in engaging a child in sexual behavior. Of course, preventing the child from telling someone is one goal not generally related to adult courtship.

The fundamental distinction, however, between child molestation and courtship is that children cannot consent to sexual activity with adults. The legal bar to a child's consent is recognition of the lack of information and power a child has in a sexual relationship with an adult. Therefore, there can be no reciprocity.

In courting behavior, the intended target of the sexual behavior has equality of knowledge and power with the person who is seeking to have sex. Grooming a child, on the other hand, is manipulation of an uninformed relatively powerless victim. Children are especially at risk due to their lack of understanding about the motives behind the acts of adults directed toward sex. Children's lack of understanding renders them extremely vulnerable to adult advances.

Although the article was about a male offender it clearly demonstrates the process of "Grooming". Grooming is not isolated to male offenders as many female offenders practice grooming as well.

PSYCHOLOGICAL PROFILE
TEENAGER / YOUNG ADULT
Fact Vs. Myth

Myth: Child Molesters spontaneously attack when they see a potential victim.

Fact: Many child molesters and pedophiles spend years positioning themselves into a place of authority and trust within the community and can spend a long time grooming one child.

> Pedophiles and child molesters behave in ways to gain a parent's trust, often ingratiating themselves with the victim's family or guardian. They often select their potential victims carefully, targeting children who are seeking adult attention. Often there is a period before the molester engages in any inappropriate behavior, and during this time the molester presents himself in a positive light, exhibits interest in the child, is complimentary, and behaves in a positive way to reassure anyone who may be suspicious of his motives (Sinclair's commentary, as cited in Schiff, 2002, ¶8).

Although this book is not primarily about Child Molesters or Pedophiles, this author theorizes that ALL predatory female behavior stems from having a sexual dysfunction from an early age.

Some examples are:

- Volunteering for positions of trust or authority wherein the perceived weaker individual or individuals will be alone with the predator. In this situation the predator can take this opportunity to either commit the act or position themselves for grooming activities aimed at gaining trust.

- Acting out towards family or friends in a more proactive way. If the predator has a child or children, they may take the opportunity to misuse or abuse the trust instinct of that child or children. In many cases, the predators own children are victimized.

- Develops a set of props or accoutrements used to either hide or assist with acts

- Has developed a routine and well developed lies in order to hide the appearance of acts upon the victim or victims

- Has a well developed internal system of denial

- Continues pathological lying

- Lack of empathy

- Shallow affection

Myth: The majority of sex crimes are reported.

Fact: Most sex crimes are not reported and therefore not prosecuted.

According to the Bureau of Justice Statistics' 2006 report on the National Crime Victimization Survey, rapes and sexual assaults of victims age 12 and older were reported to the police in 38% of cases. This varies by the relationship to the offender, with 56% of offenses involving strangers being reported, and only 28% of offenses involving non-strangers being reported. These reporting rates also vary by victim age:

Victim Age	Percent Reporting the Assault to Police
12-19	33%
20-34	30%
35-49	62%
50-64	37%

Eleven percent of child rape victims reported the crime, though not necessarily to the police (Smith, Letourneau, Saunders, Kilpatrick, Resnick & Best, 2000); 2-8% of incest victims report sexual offenses (U.S. Department of Justice, 2003).

Although 50% of violent crime victims over the age of 12 contact police, only 36% of sexual assault victims over the age of 12 report the crime to authorities (Bureau of Justice Statistics, 2005).

Studies using the polygraph ("lie detector test") have found that sex offenders have often committed sex crimes that went undisclosed and were never reported to police or child protective agencies (Ahlmeyer, Heil, McKee, & English, 2000; English, Jones, Pasini-Hill, & Cooley-Towell, 2000).

A Female Predator

Sexual Masochism

Category

<u>Paraphilias and Sexual Disorders</u>

Etiology

There are different theories related to sexual masochism, many stemming from the psychoanalytic camp. They suggest that childhood trauma (e.g., sexual abuse) or significant childhood experiences can manifest itself in exhibitionistic behavior.

Symptoms

Sexually masochistic behaviors are typically evident by early adulthood, and often start with masochistic or sadistic play in childhood. The disorder is characterized by either intense sexually arousing fantasies, urges, or behaviors in which the individual is humiliated, beaten, bound, or made to suffer in some way.

Treatment

Treatment typically involves psychotherapy aimed at uncovering and working through the underlying cause of the behavior.

Prognosis

Prognosis is good although often there are other issues which may surface once the behaviors are extinguished. If this is the case, these issues must be worked through as well.

PSYCHOLOGICAL PROFILE
ADULT
Fact Vs. Myth

Myth: All sex offenders are likely to commit another sex crime.

Fact: While any type of sexual recidivism is unacceptable, sexual recidivism vary by offender type and are lower than other types of crimes.

Background: This is a controversial area, and different studies have produced different results. Some of these different results may depend on how recidivism is defined: new criminal charges, new charges or arrest for sexual offenses, any new conviction, any new charge, or on a lesser scale, parole violations or the number of court appearances (Langevin, Curnoe, Fedoroff, Bennett, Langevin, Peever, Pettica, & Sandhu, 2004). Recidivism rates are also dependent on factors such as the sample population being observed and the amount of follow-up time after their release into the community (Greenberg, Bradford, Firestone, & Curry, 2000). And, because not all sex offenses are reported, it is difficult to accurately measure the rate of all offenses (including those that may not have been reported). 85

Early research into patterns of criminal offending revealed that a small number of offenders are responsible for a large proportion of criminal events. Wolfgang, Figlio and Sellin's (1972) classic study investigating delinquency in a birth cohort, 12.1% of offenders accounted for 84.5% of the total crime therefore, it is expected that among the sex offenders who have *not* recidivated, only a small number of pose the greatest risk.

Certain sub-types of sex offenders are at particularly high risk to reoffend. This would include individuals who exhibit high levels of sexual deviance (as measured by the penile plethysmograph or a dimension within the SVR-20) in combination with high levels of psychopathy (as measured by the Psychopathology Checklist-Revised [PCL-R]; Hare, 2004). Offenders with this combination have been shown to have sexual recidivism rates ranging between 41% (Olver & Wong, 2006) and 82% (Hildebrand, de Ruiter, & de Vogel, 2004).

The results of several studies indicate that other sub-types of sex offenders are less likely to recidivate:

One study across 15 states followed criminals for three

years after they were released from prison to see if they were rearrested for any type of crime. As a group, 43% of sex offenders were rearrested for any crime, compared to 68% for criminals who were not sex offenders. For those originally convicted of violent crimes, the rate was 62%; for property crimes the rate was 74%; for drug crimes it was 67%; and for public-order crimes the rate of re arrest was 62% (Bureau of Justice Statistics, 2003).

In the same study, while 43% of sex offenders were rearrested, only 5% of the 9,691 sex offenders released from prison were rearrested for new sex crimes within three years (Bureau of Justice Statistics, 2003). Therefore, even when sex offenders were arrested again, most of these later arrests were not for a sexual crime.

Two reviews combining results of 82 studies involving more than 29,000 sex offenders from the U.S., Canada and Europe found recidivism rates for sex crimes to be 14% over 4 to 6 years. "Recidivism" in the various studies was defined differently. Usually it was either new arrest or a new conviction; but in some studies it was measured by re incarceration, parole violations, or self-reports. (Hanson & Bussière, 1998; Hanson & Morton-Bourgon, 2005).

Over a 15-year period, sex offense re arrest rates for all sex offenders averaged 24%. While this is not insignificant, it also indicates that 3 out of 4 sex offenders are not rearrested in 15 years (Harris & Hanson, 2004).

Harris and Hanson (2004) combined the results of several studies of 4,724 sex offenders, which are summarized as follows:

Sexual Recidivism by Type of Offender

	Time Since Release Into Community		
Type of Sex Offender	5 years	10 years	15 years
Rapists	14%	21%	24%
Incest offenders	6%	9%	13%
Girl victim child molesters	9%	13%	16%
Boy victim child	23%	28%	35%

Sexual Recidivism by Type of Offender

	Time Since Release Into Community		
Type of Sex Offender	**5 years**	**10 years**	**15 years**
molesters			
Overall, All Categories of Victims and Sex Crimes:			
Offenders with no previous sexual conviction	10%	15%	19%
Offenders with a previous sexual conviction	25%	32%	37%

Note: In this study sexual recidivism was measured using the definitions from the original research reports: 5 studies used convictions, 4 studies used new charges (or a new conviction), and one sample used convictions, charges, and additional police information (Manitoba).

As noted above, because not all sex offenses are reported, it is difficult to accurately measure the true rate of repeat offenses (including reported and non-reported crimes). However, based on convictions for sex offenses, Hanson (2006) estimated the following rates of recidivism:

Estimated Sexual Recidivism Rates

Years of Follow-Up	Observed (Conviction Rate)	Estimated Re Offense Rate
5	10-15	30-40
10	15-20	30-45
20	30-40	40-55

STALKING

According to an article entitled: These boots were made for stalking, written for Innovations in Clinical Neuroscience by doctors Sarah G. West M.D and Susan Hatters Friedman M.D.:

Stalking has likely existed since the dawn of mankind, but it is only in the past several decades that the subject has appeared regularly in the psychiatric literature.[1] It was not until 1989, when the actress Rebecca Schaeffer was murdered by a stalker, that the movement to create anti stalking laws was initiated.[2] However, it is important to recognize that "stalking is not only a crime for celebrities."[3]

According to Meloy, stalking is "the willful, malicious, and repeated following or harassing of another person that threatens his or her safety."[4] Though state laws differ somewhat, this behavior is illegal in all 50 states.[5] Large community surveys indicate that the lifetime risk for becoming the victim of stalking for a man is two percent and for a woman is eight percent.[6,7]

In 1999, Mullen, et al.,[8] published a landmark study based on a population of

145 stalkers referred to a forensic psychiatric clinic. The sample consisted of 115 men and 30 women. Researchers examined the duration and methods associated with the stalking, the occurrence of threats and violence, the relationship of the stalker to the victims, and the psychiatric status and criminal histories of the stalker. From their data, the authors derived the following typology for classifying stalkers, which aids in understanding the range of motivations for the behavior.

TABLE 1. Mullen's stalker typology[8]

The Rejected Stalker—stalking follows the end of a relationship

The Intimacy Seeking Stalker—stalking based on a desire for intimacy

The Incompetent Stalker—stalking with lack of social skills; stalker feels entitled to a relationship

The Resentful Stalker—stalking meant to frighten victims

The Predatory Stalker—stalking in preparation for a sexual attack

Which leads to a discussion of Stalkers Types. According to doctors West and Friedman there are five stalker types:

The rejected stalker. This was the largest group (n=52), and their behavior was brought about by the termination of a relationship, most commonly with a romantic partner, but also with estranged mothers, broken friendships, or strained work relationships. Often, these stalkers experienced ambivalent feelings about reconciliation and revenge regarding their targets. The majority suffered from personality disorders, although about one-fifth had delusional disorders. This group had the widest range of methods associated with stalking but was significantly associated with telephone harassment.

The intimacy seeking stalker. This group was also large (n=49). Classification was based on the desire for intimacy with someone that the stalkers had identified as their true love.

Half believed that their love was requited, qualifying for the Diagnositc and Statistical Manual of Mental Disorders, Fourth Edition (DSM-IV) diagnosis of delusional disorder, erotomanic type.[9] The other half were termed to have morbid infatuations, in which they recognized that their love was not returned but "insist(ed), with delusional intensity, on both the legitimacy and the eventual success of their quest."[10] Along with the rejected stalkers, this group tended to be the most persistent over time.

The incompetent stalker. These stalkers (n=22) lacked appropriate social skills and knowledge of courtship rituals but hoped that, regardless of these deficits, their behavior would lead to intimacy. These stalkers targeted people that they believed would be good romantic partners but were not infatuated with them to the same degree as the intimacy seekers. They too did not believe that their feelings were reciprocated, but rather that they were entitled to a relationship. This group had often stalked other victims before.

The resentful stalker. This category (n=16) included those stalkers whose behaviors were meant to distress and frighten their victims. Half acted on grievances against specific people, while the others were generally disgruntled and chose targets at random. In addition to the rejected group, these stalkers were most likely to threaten their victims.

The predatory stalker. While most notorious, this was the smallest group (n=6) and contained only men. These stalkers acted in preparation for a sexual attack. They enjoyed the power inherent in their stalking behavior. They were predominantly diagnosed with paraphilias and were the most likely to have prior convictions for sexual offenses.

Also:

Battered women who stalk. A study focusing on stalking and unwanted pursuit behavior perpetrated by 55 women residing in a battered women's shelter was published in 2006.[21] A limitation of this study, as described by the authors, involved an inability to ask the subjects, due to the concerns of the shelter employees, about their motivations for perpetrating the stalking behavior.

The women, on average, were in their early 30s, were unemployed, and had children. The specific acts perpetrated by this group of women included begging the abuser not to leave, seeking information from others about the abuser, giving the abuser unwanted gifts, visiting the abuser unexpectedly, following the abuser, making a threat toward the abuser, or threatening suicide or self-harm. It was noted that, if these women had themselves previously been a victim of these behaviors, they were more likely to become a perpetrator of similar behavior. These women were more likely to form insecure attachments, suffer from depression, blame themselves for the abuse, and leave the shelter quickly compared to other women in the shelter who did not participate in stalking or unwanted pursuit behavior.

The Research on Female Stalkers

International survey study. Meloy and Boyd[19] collected data on 82 adult women who had engaged in stalking behavior via a survey sent to mental health and law enforcement professionals in the United States, Canada, and Australia. Though this study has some limitations, including a dependence on the observations of a variety of clinicians who were not using a standardized instrument to evaluate the female subjects, it assesses one of the large groups of female stalkers found in the literature.

Typically, the perpetrators were Caucasian, heterosexual, single women with a mean age of 35 (ranging from 18–58 years old). Often, these women did not have children. They appeared to be educated, with a large majority having graduated from high school and a solid minority having achieved a college or graduate degree. Their intelligence may have allowed them to be more successful in pursuing their victims.

Reports of substance abuse were not common, but about one-third of women used substances while stalking. Available data suggested the presence of Axis I and II disorders. Twenty percent of those with Axis I disorders were diagnosed with delusional disorder. The most common Axis II diagnosis was borderline personality disorder (n=10 of 22). Antisocial personality disorder was not diagnosed in any of the women. Despite incomplete data, there appeared to be a high rate of sexual (n=18 of 40) and physical (n=12 of 40) abuse in the personal histories of the female stalkers, which may have predisposed these women to the development of borderline personality characteristics or posttraumatic stress disorder.

A great majority of the victims of female stalkers were known to them, either as acquaintances, former lovers, or family members. However, one-fifth of the victims were completely unknown to their stalkers. Frequent reasons for stalking included anger, obsession, feelings of abandonment, loneliness, and dependency. Usual stalking behaviors included telephone calls and messages, giving letters and gifts, driving by the victim's location, trespassing, and following the victim. More than half of the women threatened their victims, and a quarter were physically violent, with three victims losing their lives to their stalkers. Most episodes of violence, however, did not involve the use of a weapon and did not result in injuries. Violence was more likely if the stalker and the victim had been previously sexually intimate. In more than half of the cases, the behavior increased in frequency and intensity. The victims were usually Caucasian, heterosexual males with a mean age of 41 (ranging from 16–68 years). Female victims were targeted one third of the time. The perpetrators pursued their victims for an average of 22 months.

Australian forensic clinic study. In 2001, Purcell, et al.,[20] published a study that compared female stalkers (n=40) to their male counterparts (n=150). The data was collected based on referrals to a community forensic mental health clinic that specializes in the assessment of stalkers. One of the limitations of this study is that it involved a retrospective analysis of data collected from evaluations performed over a period of eight years.

Similar to the men, the women, on average, were 35 years old, single, and employed. Women were less likely to have a history of criminal behavior. Almost half of the women (n=18 of 40) had an Axis I diagnosis, most commonly (10 of 18) delusional disorder. Half (n=20 of 40) were diagnosed with an Axis II disorder, including borderline, dependent, and narcissistic personality disorders. The diagnostic profiles of these women did not differ from their male counterparts, except women had lower rates of substance use.

With only two exceptions, female stalkers knew their victims. Forty percent of the victims were professional contacts, frequently mental health professionals. Men were comparatively more likely to pursue strangers. Same gender stalking was more frequent among women than men. Based on Mullen's typology,[8] women's primary motive for stalking behavior in almost half of the cases was to seek intimacy. In the female group, there were no cases of sexually motivated predatory stalking, which differed from the male stalkers. Women and men appeared to stalk their victims for a similar duration of time. Women were more likely to harass their victims via telephone call but less likely to physically pursue them when compared to men. Strikingly, women had the same propensity to make threats and become violent, including property damage and assault, as the male stalkers.

LAPD study. In an effort to determine the degree of intimacy in the stalker-victim relationship, Palarea, et al.,[22] compared 135 intimate and 88 nonintimate stalkers investigated by the Los Angeles Police Department's Threat Management Unit. Women accounted for 22 percent of the sample. Unfortunately, despite a large amount of data collected on this group, not much of it was analyzed specifically by gender. Intimate stalkers were married to, engaged to, cohabited with, dated, or had a casual sexual relationship with the victim. The authors determined that women were somewhat more likely to participate in no intimate stalking (n=28 of 49 or 57.1%) when compared to intimate stalking. This differed from the men, who were more likely to be suspects in the intimate stalking cases (n=114 of 174 or 65.5%).

Case reports. There have been a number of interesting case reports published on female stalkers. The first case highlights a potential etiology for stalking behavior. Soliman, et al.,[23] described a woman diagnosed with Huntington's disease exhibiting escalating stalking behavior directed toward her female therapist. This was accompanied by amorous feelings toward and obsessive thoughts about this therapist. Her behaviors included frequent phone calls, unwanted gifts, threats, and physical assault. The stalking behavior in this patient may have been linked to caudate dysfunction caused by the Huntington's disease. Basal ganglia lesions may have accounted for the obsessive thoughts and amorous feelings. Her thoughts and behavior resolved following treatment with a selective serotonin reuptake inhibitor (SSRI) and an antipsychotic. This case supports the theory that stalking behavior may be caused by an increase in subcortical dopaminergic function and a decrease in serotonergic activity.[24]

According to another case report, therapy addressing psychodynamic issues may be an effective treatment for stalkers. A 34-year-old woman requested to see a psychiatrist after disclosing to her primary care physician her long-standing history of stalking behavior.[25] She had been following an older female colleague who held a superior position at her place of employment. The patient followed this woman to her home but denied any violent or sexual fantasies about her. The patient described she had a similar obsession concerning a female teacher from the ages of 12 to 16. Additionally, she had previously been terminated by a female therapist who was the target of similar thoughts and behaviors. The patient's history revealed that she was adopted and had a twin whose personality was described as outgoing and exuberant and with whom she had little contact. She discovered the existence of her twin at age seven, at which point it was confirmed by her adoptive mother and never mentioned again. The patient chose not to contact her biological mother for fear that it would distress her adoptive mother. On examination, the patient did not fulfill DSM diagnostic criteria for obsessive compulsive disorder, a delusional disorder, or a personality disorder. Psychodynamically, it was postulated that she was looking for a maternal figure and role model in the women that she followed. After she agreed to cease this behavior, she was referred to a male therapist for ongoing psychotherapy around these issues.

In 2006, Reisner[26] published a case report on a female stalker with multiple psychiatric diagnoses, including Munchausen syndrome by proxy (MSBP) and borderline personality disorder. The patient lost custody of her two young children after it became evident that she harmed her older child in a manner consistent with MSBP. She later admitted to overdosing him on diphenylhydantoin and injecting him with soda or saliva. While she was being investigated for this behavior, she began stalking the child protective service worker who was assigned to her case. She allegedly harassed the case worker through the internet and threatened to kill her; for this, she was charged with aggravated menacing. She received intense psychiatric treatment and responded well to clozapine and, later, quetiapine.

As indicated earlier, clinicians not only treat stalkers and their victims, but they may also find themselves the targets of stalking behavior. Another report described a female patient who presented to a family practice group complaining of depression and was prescribed a one-week supply of an antidepressant. She took the pills all at once and went to the emergency room, where a computed tomography (CT) scan revealed brain atrophy. She erroneously believed that this was caused by her primary care provider. She called this doctor's medical practice numerous times, day and night. She loitered in the office building that housed the practice. She made false allegations about a sexual assault involving her physician, and she threatened to kill her physician. Ultimately, both police and the medical board assisted in establishing firm boundaries to prevent the continuation of this behavior.

TABLE 4. Common characteristics of female stalkers

Caucasian
Heterosexual
Single
Age in mid-30s
Without children
Educated
Employed
Lack of substance abuse
Axis I and II disorders common
Victims often known to them
Threats and violence possible

Female Celebrity Stalkers and Hollywood

In 1949, Eddie Waitkus, a 29-year-old first baseman for the Philadelphia Phillies, was lured to a hotel room and shot by Ruth Ann Steinhagen, a fan who had been obsessed with him for a number of years.[27] Public personas, such as athletes, actors, and television personalities, are a common target for stalkers. This may be because "the mentally ill will develop delusions about whatever is in their environment, and television became an important part of the environment, bringing new people and new faces into their lives."[28] Female stalkers are no exception to this. David Letterman, long-time host of late night television, was plagued by the stalking behavior of Margaret Ray, a mentally ill woman who ultimately committed suicide in 1998.[29] Brad Pitt[30] and John Cusack[31] have also been prey to female stalkers. According to Mullen, et al., most celebrity stalkers resemble the rejected or intimacy seeking stalker.[32]

Hollywood has capitalized on the phenomenon of female stalkers. Fatal Attraction, a 1987 film, concerns a man who has a one-night stand with a woman who stalks him and terrorizes his family. Misery, a novel by Stephen King that was later made into a film, tells the story of an obsessive female fan of an author who abducts him after his car crashes and then tortures him under the guise of caring for him. Single White Female, a 1992 film, describes a woman who becomes obsessed with her roommate to the point where she assumes her identity. In Wicker Park, a 2004 film, the male protagonist may have been stalked by a woman (but we don't want to give away the ending).[33]

Relevance to Mental Health Professionals

In addition to being called upon to treat both stalkers and their victims, there is another important reason that mental health professionals should be familiar with the characteristics of stalking: mental health professionals may themselves become victims of stalkers. Research demonstrates that, in a variety of samples, 11 percent of mental health professionals have been the victims of stalking (a weighted mean with a range of 3–29%).[11–15] Stalkers who targeted mental health professionals Table 2 were typically male with a major mental disorder diagnosed on Axis I and a comorbid personality disorder on Axis II. They may also have had a prior history of stalking behavior.[16] The stalker was frequently under the direct care of the victim, and the motive was often a desire for greater intimacy.[11]

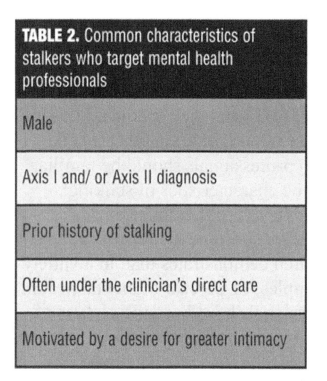

TABLE 2. Common characteristics of stalkers who target mental health professionals

Male
Axis I and/ or Axis II diagnosis
Prior history of stalking
Often under the clinician's direct care
Motivated by a desire for greater intimacy

Of all the mental health professionals, psychiatrists and psychologists were the most likely to be stalked; this may be related to a patient's potential to misconstrue boundaries and assign an inappropriate amount of intimacy to his or her therapeutic relationship with the practitioner.[11] Clinicians who are stalked must be wary not to minimize their patients' behavior and to also recognize that the stalkers may pose a serious threat (Table 3).[16] Certain prodromal behaviors, such as requests for personal information or chance meetings outside the office setting, should be noted. It is useful to systematically document this and other suspicious activities, such as gifts or unusual phone messages, in a separate file along with the dates and times at which they occurred.[17,18] All of this information should also be reported in team meetings or supervision.[11]

In order to discourage potential stalkers, clinicians should carefully protect their private information (e.g., home address, cell phone numbers). If stalking is suspected, consultation with forensic specialists, the police, or lawyers may be necessary. It may also be necessary to alert one's own family to the threat, given that their safety may be in jeopardy. A restraining order may be another alternative, though they are not always effective.

Conclusion

Women who stalk may make headlines as celebrity stalkers or as the subject of Hollywood films. However, these behaviors are not simply limited to the popular press. In general, female stalkers tend to be single and in their mid-30s and may carry diagnoses on both Axis I and Axis II. A common Axis I diagnosis is delusional disorder, which requires a belief that the object of the woman's affection reciprocates her feelings of love. Borderline personality disorder is a frequently mentioned diagnosis on Axis II.

Female stalkers tend to target people that they know, and they are capable of threatening their victims and even becoming violent. We must be cautious not to underestimate women's potential for violence secondary to a gender bias. Though there are a variety of motives for their behavior, women do not often engage in sexually predatory behavior. Finally, mental health professionals should be aware of the possibility of female stalkers in both their clinical practice and their personal life, as stalkers may target their care providers.

Although a case is made for Mental Health Professionals and law enforcement to be stalked more than the average person, I believe this is false and that most predatory behavior goes un reported and even un noticed until the moment of contact is made overwhelmingly obvious to the victim. Usually at which time the stalker's urges to make contact are no longer controllable.

TABLE 3. Tips for mental health professionals who may become the target of a stalker

Guard personal information carefully

Be aware of patients' boundary violations, such as the following:
- Requests for personal information
- Unusual phone calls or messages
- Frequent and inappropriate gifts
- Contact outside of work setting

Record all unusual activity

Report unusual activity to supervisors

Consult with specialists

Alert one's family to the threat

Consider a restraining order against the perpetrator

TABLE 4. Common characteristics of female stalkers

Caucasian
Heterosexual
Single
Age in mid-30s
Without children
Educated
Employed
Lack of substance abuse
Axis I and II disorders common
Victims often known to them
Threats and violence possible

According to another article entitled: "The dangers of online stalking" for the blog ItaliaGregory "You could be a victim and not even know it yet". With so many users on sites like FACEBOOK, MEEBO, LINKDIN and TWITTER it makes it easier than ever for the once clever online stalker to figure out where you are and exactly what you're doing without having to do much additional work, if any. Now, the term, "Stalker" is used loosely in today's society, but here I'm not talking about the girl that checks her ex bf's FACEBOOK page every day just to see what he's up to. I'm talking about when it becomes an obsession and could potentially become a dangerous situation.

While the stalking may easily start online, it can quickly escalate to the point that the person becomes infatuated with the idea of watching your every move. While most people picture stalkers to typically be men, don't underestimate the power of women! Here's a rundown if you're ever wearily about a person having stalker potential:

1. Jealous

2. Narcissistic

3. Obsessive and compulsive

4. Falls "instantly" in love

5. Manipulative

6. Does not take responsibility for own feelings or actions

7. Needs to have control over others

8. Socially awkward or uncomfortable

9. Views self as a victim of society, family, and others

10. Unable to take "no" for an answer

11. Deceptive

12. Often switches between rage and "love"

13. Difficulty distinguishing between fantasy and reality

14. Sense of entitlement ("You owe me...")

15. Unable to cope with rejection

16. Dependent on others for sense of "self"

17. Views his or her problems as someone else's fault

18. May be above average intelligence

Source: Spence-Diehl. Stalking: A Handbook for Victims

Schizoaffective Disorder

Category

Psychotic Disorders

Etiology

Most theories suggest a biological component for this disorder, much like for schizophrenia.

Symptoms

The term schizoaffective implies a combination of schizophrenia and an affective (or mood) disorder, which is actually quite accurate. Symptoms include those for schizophrenia (see above) as well as a Major Depressive, manic, or mixed episode (see mood disorders). The psychotic (or schizophrenic like symptoms) must be present without any disturbance in mood for a minimum of two weeks.

Treatment

Treatment typically involves medication to treat both the psychotic and affective symptoms. Therapy can be helpful in terms of increasing interpersonal skills, insight into the illness and need for medication. Assistance with occupational issues can also be beneficial.

Prognosis

There is no cure for this disorder so prognosis is poor. However, medication has been shown to be quite effective against the psychotic symptoms and therapy can help the individual cope with the illness better and improve social functioning. Absence of what is termed the negative symptoms (flatted affect, avolition, and poor social interaction) improves the prognosis significantly.

MONSTRVM ROMÆ INVENTVM MORTVVM
IN TIBERI. ANNO 1496.

Was Gott selbs von dem Bapstum helt/
Zeigt dis schrecklich Bild hie gestelt.
Dafür jederman grawen solt/
Wenn ers zu hertzen nemen wolt.

Mart. Luther D.

1545.

Frotteurism

Category

Paraphilias and Sexual Disorders

Etiology

Like most disorders in this category, many theories exist in an attempt to explain how this disorder develops. Most experts agree that there are underlying issues related to childhood which play a major role in the etiology.

Symptoms

This disorder is characterized by either intense sexually arousing fantasies, urges, or behaviors in which the individual touches or rubs against an non-consenting person in a sexual manner. This often occurs in somewhat conspicuous situations such as on a crowded bus or subway. To be considered diagnosable, the fantasies, urges, or behaviors must cause significant distress in the individual or be disruptive to his or her everyday functioning.

Treatment

Treatment typically involves psychotherapy aimed at uncovering and working through the underlying cause of the behavior.

Prognosis

Prognosis is good although often there are other issues which may surface once the behaviors are extinguished. If this is the case, these issues must be worked through as well.

THREATENING / HARASSMENT

In the case of threatening behavior an or harassment type behavior, whether passive aggressive or outright, most often is the behavior of a female predator. Whether it begins in the pre verbal stage, aggressively develops itself during pre adolescence and teenage years only to present itself, full force throughout the adult lifespan. Part of the threat matrix we have found will undoubtedly be thus:

Harassment through:
Manipulation
As part of the predators learned skill, she quickly takes a mental and physical assessment of her chosen prey, thus using psychological manipulation to try and control her subject (s).

Threats Used:

Blackmail usually professional or personal

As part of a female predators behavior we have found that a part of threat matrix usually involves blackmail. Often times the predator will say, "You better not say, or do, that or else, I'll tell so and so you are or you did something bad." There needs not be any proof or that it have any bearing in reality to be true at all, so long as the predator thinks it and projects it upon her chosen subject, to her, it becomes real. If the subject is very small such as a pre adolescent child, image how profound a technique this can be. Alternatively, adult women, girls and teenagers are also subject to this.

PHYSICAL ATTACKS / MURDER

In the case of physical attacks, I don't like to use the term "rarely" when I say they do not usually lead to murder. However, the countless women and children who've lost their lives at the hands of a female predator are innumerable and is quite a number that should be respected. Also a part of a female predators modus operandi is the "physical attack". Never can she be seen without it, its part of her nature and she will go to extreme lengths to play it out.

Case in point I used to have a friend named Carlie. We were standing in line purchasing items when she noticed a little girl, who I imagine couldn't have been more than 2 years old. Carlie says to me, "Ugh! Look at her, she looks crazy!!" Now, I looked at the toddler she was attacking, I looked at the mother, I looked around me at the people standing closely to us. I responded, "What? She's a baby, why would you say that?" to which Carlie responded incredulously, "She just looks crazy!!" That was the absolute end of that friendship. I have neither spoken with nor have I ever seen this woman again. But from this example you can clearly see this adult woman lashing out at a defenseless little girl, under the age of 5.

Physical attacks do not usually end in murder, but they often times end in violence or perpetuate violence. The physical attack could also be played out verbally, such as the example I have just given. A recent scientific study performed by Sarah Gervais, assistant professor of psychology at the University of Nebraska-Lincoln found that women also aggressively look at and objectify the bodies of other females regardless of age.

The study results were published in the European Journal of Social Psychology and examined the different ways people process images of men and women.

According to the study, men tend to be processed on a "global" level, in which their entire physical being is viewed as a whole. Women tend to be viewed much differently, by what the study calls "local" cognitive processing, in which women are measured as a collection of various body parts.

"Local processing underlies the way we think about objects: houses, cars and so on. But global processing should prevent us from that when it comes to people," Gervais told Science Daily.

"We don't break people down to their parts—except when it comes to women, which is really striking. Women were perceived in the same ways that objects are viewed." Could Carlie have been using this type of cognitive processing on that small child?

AGGRAVATED SEXUAL ASSAULT

In the case of aggravated sexual assault, a common part of female predatory behavior there are many types and sub categories. Many people like to dispel that women and girls engage in aggravated sexual assault, but given these examples we begin to understand how very common it is.

What is sexual assault in the first place? Sexual assault, is the sexual violation or sexual molestation of any individual. What is aggravated sexual assault mean? Let's just say, it's stabbing a person and then, turning the knife counter clockwise, pulling it out slowly, sharpening it and then jabbing it back in repeatedly. It's essentially the reckless disregard of the person and when you join the words, Aggravated and Sexual Assault, you begin to understand why this is so devastating. The different types of Aggravated

Sexual Assault can range from what others outside of the victim may view as "harmless play" to what a consensus would agree upon as being totally unacceptable. Among many adults its widely acceptable for women to openly touch and or fondle each other and otherwise show sensual attention even in public places, even among teenagers and very small children. However, this is not necessarily normal behavior and may not be preferred or even practiced by all females regardless of age.

In fact, many women may secretly feel put off or disgusted by this type of behavior and just the opposite, many women may be turned on by or lean into perpetrating this type of behavior on others regardless of negative responses from those who do not wish it.

Aggravated sexual assault can from an outside viewer pass as something benign because of this widely accepted notion that "Girls are more touchy feely than men." Some of the more passive types or lesser forms of sexual assault called sexual battery can be that the predator constantly:

Sniffs or breathes in another woman's scent, she may get up close to do this or take the opportunity to do so in close quarters

Constantly offer up opportunities to touch another woman or girls hair and verbally obsesses over it

Constantly offers compliments and observations on other women's, girls bodies and offers opportunities or capitalizes upon opportunities to view the subject naked or to watch the subject un robe. Added to this, may be manipulation techniques. "You look so good, you really should try this." And the predator touches the subject. Or "You really need to loose more weight." And the Predator emotionally blackmails the subject.

If the subject is suffering from a mental illness or co-occurring drug abuse or alcohol problem any one of these could be a triggering event and introduce a different set of complex problems.

Ultimately this type of sexual battery goes on as part of the routine assault procedure of the female predator and usually only gets worse. Sexual battery is a precursor to Sexual Assault and Aggravated Sexual Assault.

The predator is actively "Seeking" to involve herself in a sexual behavior with another women, girl or child. Usually, these sexualized feelings for other women are repressed at best and the passive type of sexual assault, sexual battery is usually a way for the female predator to safely satisfy her desire.

Antoinette Davis & Mario Andrette McNeil

Shaniya Davis

CASE STUDIES
WOMEN WHO KILL CHILDREN
TANDEM KILLERS

On or around November 10th 2009 Antoinette Davis reported her five year old daughter Shaniya Davis missing. Later that day, a surveillance camera in a hotel 30 miles away showed a man carrying a girl matching Shaniya's description. Police identified the man as Mario Andrette McNeill. On November 13, McNeill was charged with first-degree kidnapping. According to court documents, McNeil murdered Shaniya on November 10th the very first day she was reported missing. According to a police report Antoinette Davis allegedly sold her daughter as a sex slave. Investigators said Antoinette Davis gave McNeil the child to pay for a drug debt.

On Wednesday July 6th 2011, Antoinette Davis was charged with first degree murder, indecent liberties with a child, child abuse, sexual servitude, rape of a child, sexual offense of a child by adult offender, human trafficking and misdemeanor making false police report.

For their crimes we place Antoinette Davis and Mario A. McNeil respectively at number 14 and 17. Firstly number 14 as a Ruthlessly Self Centered Psychopathic Schemer who kills to benefit him/herself. Secondly number 17 as a Sexually Perverse Serial Murderer where rape is the primary motive and the victim is killed to hide the evidence.

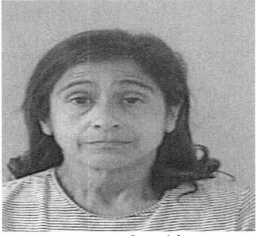

Nancy Garrido

Jaycee Dugard

Nancy Garrido

On June 10th 1991, Nancy Garrido aided her husband Phillip Garrido in stalking, physically assaulting by use of a stun gun, abducted, falsely imprisoned, raped and committed physical and psychological torture on eleven year old Jaycee Dugar for eighteen years until being discovered by police officers on August 26th 2009.

During this time, Nancy assisted Phillip and "prepared" Jaycee for rape by ritualistically bathing her. Nancy groomed Jaycee by using psychological methods of influence, threats, intimidation and manipulation. It is said that Nancy was chiefly responsible for "scouting" the girls as "prizes" for her husband. A video tape showing Nancy Garrido video tapping girls as young as 4 years old in a public park and one showing Nancy Garrido coercing a five year old girl to show her private parts while secretly video tapping her were publicized after her conviction. After her conviction Nancy could be seen in a police interrogation video, confessing that she indeed was trying to get as many shots of the girls private parts for her husband as she could.

For this crime we have placed Nancy Garrido at number 3 on Dr. Stone's scale of evil as a willing companion of a killer, but she is also at times a number 17, someone who is sexually perverse and at other times a number 22, a psychopath who inflicts extreme torture on their victims.

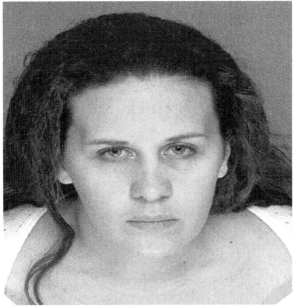

Melissa Huckaby

Sandra Cantu

CASE STUDIES
WOMEN WHO KILL CHILDREN
SOLITARY KILLERS

Melissa Huckaby

Once a Christian Sunday school teacher, she taught children the ropes, how to be good people in life. She taught kids the Christian principals of "Thou shall not kill" and "Thou shall not covet they neighbors wife". Rightly so, shouldn't the latter also cover thy neighbors children?

On or around March 27th 2009, 28 year old Melissa Huckaby, stalked, coerced, kidnapped, tortured, raped and killed eight year old Sandra Cantu in Tracy California. According to the Tracy California police pathology report, Melissa Murdered Sandra Cantu inside her grandfather's church. Melissa, using torn fabric, fashioned a noose and strangled Sandra. Also, according to the report Melissa used a rolling pin, to brutally beat and sexually assault (aggravated sexual assault) eight year old Sandra Cantu. We theorize Melissa wanted to punish Sandra and may even have objectified Sandra as a kind of "doll". Naturally, Melissa did not have to try hard to coerce Sandra, seeing as Sandra knew Melissa as the mother of her childhood friend. Asking the question of why Melissa asphyxiated Sandra with a noose? A noose is something one needs to fashion, so the implication here is one of a very determined person intent on subjecting one to suffering.

Why did Melissa use a rolling pin to brutally beat Sandra? It would seem that Melissa wanted to punish Sandra for something real or unreal, whatever, Melissa thought in her mind to rationalize her actions.

Why did Melissa sexually assault Sandra? Melissa seemed to objectify Sandra as a doll, separating any semblance of humanity from the child and using her we theorize as a kind of "experiment".

While in court Melissa Huckaby denied ever raping Sandra and claimed that Sandra "never suffered" and that she never meant for Sandra to suffer. However, the pathology report claims otherwise, citing bloody bruises and marks injuries consistent with beating, asphyxiation and rape. Certainly, it sounds like one would suffer from such things. The pathology report in the case of Sandra Cantu was brutal and to graphic to discuss here. Surely, this little girl was made to suffer at the hands of a female predator.

For her crimes, we place Melissa Huckaby at number 17 on the scale of Dr. Eli Stone's scale of evil as a sexually perverse murder.

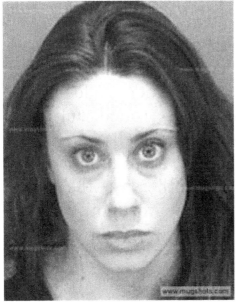

Casey Anthony

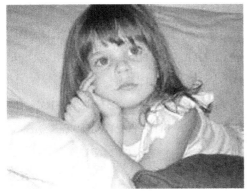

Caylee Anthony

Casey Anthony

On or around June 16th 2008 the Casey Anthony failed to notify anyone that she had not seen her child Caylee Anthony all day. Around July 15th Casey Anthony finally tells her mother that she had not seen her child all month. Casey's mother was the person actually responsible for notifying the police that her little grand daughter had been missing for over a month. On December 11th 2008 Caylee Anthony's remains were found in a wooded area near a road not far from Casey Anthony's home. On October 14, 2008, Casey Anthony was indicted by a grand jury on charges of first degree murder, aggravated child abuse, aggravated manslaughter of a child, and four counts of providing false information to police. Although to this very day Casey denies ever knowing what happened to her child, we theorize that Caylee drowned in her bathtub, although, it had been theorized that Caylee drowned in the backyard pool.

For her crimes Casey Anthony is placed at number 11 as a psychopathic killer who murder people who are in the way.

Lori Drew

Megan Meier

Lori Drew

During the summer of 2006, Lori, who lived with her teenaged daughter became concerned that her daughter's friend Megan Meier was spreading false statements about her daughter. Lori, her daughter, and one of Lori's employees, Ashley Grills, allegedly decided to create a MySpace account for a non-existent 16-year-old boy with the alias "Josh Evans" and to use that account to discover whether Megan was spreading rumors about Lori's daughter.

In September 2006, Lori used this fake MySpace account to contact Megan. Megan, believing the ruse, decided to converse with this "Josh Evans" for about a month through October 2006 via MySpace in a manner the prosecution described as "flirtatious". On or about October 16th 2006, "Josh Evans" sent a message to Megan suggesting she should kill herself and that the world would be a better place without her. Its been reported that Megan not only received suicide suggestions from "Josh Evans" but that she began to receive a barrage of negative messages from other MySpace users all having ties to this one "Josh Evans". Shortly after thirteen year old Megan Meier, was found by her mother, hanging in her bedroom closet, Megan had committed suicide. After Megan's death, Lori Drew deleted the fake MySpace account she'd created under the alias, "Josh Evans" and intimidated a witness into keeping silent.

For her crimes Lori Drew is placed at number 10 as a non-psychopathic killer who kills people who are in the way.

Stephanie, Andy and Steven Lopez

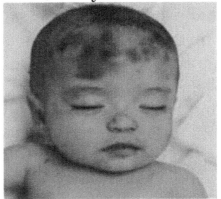

Brianna Lopez

CASE STUDIES
WOMEN WHO KILL CHILDREN
GROUP MURDERES

The Murder of Baby Brianna

Baby Brianna, as she is still so lovingly referred to was a beautiful, healthy six month old baby girl who was savagely beaten, tortured, raped and murdered by her mother who was assisted by her husband and brother in 2002. According to the Las Cruces New Mexico District Attorney Susana Martinez "They raped her; they beat her. She had bite marks on her face, cheek, head, arms, legs, chest, torso, everywhere. Literally bruised from head to toe, from the top of her head all throughout her body all the way to the big toe on her right foot."

According to Detective Lindell Wright the first officer on the scene, "Massive bruising on the head, and then her little fingers were lacerated, toes. Later, when he had time to look back, I cried my eyes out. It will stay with me for the rest of my life."

According to investigators, "Brianna's mother and father, Stephanie Lopez and Andy Walters, and her uncle Steven Lopez were responsible.

The night before, Steven and Andy threw Brianna to the ceiling, then let her slam to the ground. And they had raped her time and time again.

Brianna's mother had bitten her child. The source of the other bruises remains a mystery.

"Bite marks throughout her body; there were old and new," Wright said. "She had skull fractures that were old and new."

"She had bleeding on the brain both old and new which means she had been abused physically her entire life."

And while all the abuse was going on another uncle and a grandmother knew but never reported it or tried to stop it." (Long term silent witness)

For their crimes we place Stephanie, Andy and Steven Lopez cumulatively at 17 and 22 on Dr. Eli Stone's scale of evil.

Karla Homolka

Tammy Homolka

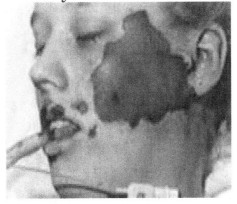

CASE STUDIES
WOMEN WHO KILL ADULTS
TANDEM KILLERS

Karla Homolka

On December 23rd 1990, once vibrant Tammy Homolka was drugged, raped and murdered by her sister Karla Homolka and Paul Bernardo. Karla Homolka is a convicted Canadian serial killer who in 1991 and 1992 raped and murdered two teenage girls, Leslie Mahaffy and Kristen French.

During a plea deal following her arrest in 1993, Karla stated she was the battered wife of Paul Bernardo and claimed that Paul was coercive of her and the main instigator who directed the events. However, video tape surfaced of the murders that showed Karla taking an active role in rape and murder of those women. According to Paul Bernardo's testimony, given to police at the time, "On 23 December 1990, "after a Homolka family Christmas party, Bernardo and Karla Homolka drugged Tammy Homolka with the animal tranquilizers. Bernardo and Karla Homolka raped Tammy while she was unconscious. Tammy later choked on her own vomit and died. Bernardo told police he tried to revive her, but failed, and her death was ruled an accident."[7] Before calling 911, they hid the evidence, redressed Tammy, who had a chemical burn on her face, and moved her into her basement bedroom."

A few hours later Tammy was pronounced dead at St. Catharine's General Hospital without having regained consciousness.

On 15 June 1991, two weeks before his wedding, Bernardo met Leslie Mahaffy, at the door of her Burlington home. Leslie had just attended the wake of her friend who had died in a car crash, it was around 2 a.m. The two spoke for some time and went back to Bernardo's car for a cigarette, at which point he forced her into the car and drove her to his house. There, Homolka and Bernardo held Leslie Mahaffy hostage for 24 hours, repeatedly sexually assaulting her. They recorded the assaults on videotape, including one scene in which Homolka pretties herself for the camera before raping the girl. Eventually, they killed her.

Karla lied about not having killed Leslie, that it was Bernardo who'd strangled her, however, Bernardo fingered Karla as the murderer, claiming she had given Leslie a lethal shot of a drug called Halcoin. Later on they put her body into the basement until they could decide how to get rid of it.

The following day Karla's parents had visited for a Father's Day family dinner.

After they ate, Karla and Paul cut up Leslie's body and disposed of it in cement blocks. Bernardo dismembered the body with a circular saw in the basement. Leslie's body parts were then encased in cement and dumped in a lake.

On June 29, a couple canoeing on the lake at the edge of St. Catharine's found the cement blocks, one of which had split open. In a truly callus and macabre fashion, Karla and Paul were married in a lavish ceremony at a nearby lake.

On April 16 1992, Karla stalked coerced, intimidated, sexually assaulted, physically assaulted and tortured over three days and then murdered Kristen French. Karla and Paul drove into a St. Catharine's church parking lot, having spotted Kristen French. Karla pretended to be lost, and asked for directions from French. Paul then forced her into the car with a knife. Karla and Paul took French to Port

Dalhousie, where for three days they sexually assaulted, abused, and tortured her. Karla blamed Paul and Paul blamed Karla. Paul claimed that Karla had beaten Kristen with a mallet as she tried to escape, and she was strangled on a noose tied around her neck secured to a hope chest. Homolka immediately left to blow-dry her hair.

For her crimes Karla Homolka is placed at number 17 and also at number 22. For her extreme callousness toward her victims, she is a sexually perverse serial murderer and a psychopath who inflicts extreme torture upon victims and then murders them.

Although Karla Homolka is a most despicable kind of female predator, she is not alone in her debauchery. It is theorized that many women, who if not apprehended and brought attention to, would recidivate.

Amanda Knox

Meredith Kercher

Amanda Knox

Amanda Knox a Seattleite and once popular student at the University of Washington allegedly killed Meredith Kercher while studying abroad in Perugia Italy on November 1st 2007. Amanda was 20 years old. Meredith was 21. The Theorized Modus Operandi for Amanda was that Amanda stalked, groomed, performed aggravated sexual assault, physically attacked and then killed Meredith in tandem with the help of her then boyfriend Raffaele Sollecito.

This places Amanda Knox at number 17 on Dr. Eli Stone's Scale of Evil. According to the scale, persons placed at number 17 are considered to be sexually perverse serial murders. Although Amanda was stopped before she could allegedly kill anyone else, it is theorized that Amanda was a thrill seeking sexually perverse killer and that was only getting started; had she been allowed to murder in silence, it is believed this would've bolstered her, giving her confidence to do it again. Not much is publically known about Amanda's early life. It was widely reported that while at the Perugia police station, Amanda performed somersaults, high kicks and laughing. There is a widely circulated picture of Amanda passionately kissing her then boyfriend Raffaello outside of the crime scene. Amanda appeared to be aroused by the murder and the attention. Although Amanda Knox was ultimately released and her case overturned, we truly believe that Amanda Knox is a female predator.

rep.L

Meredith Kercher Crime Scene

rep.E

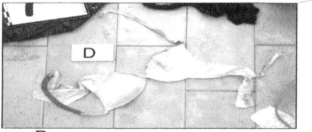

rep.D

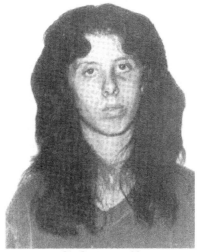

Judith Neelley

Lisa Ann Millican

CASE STUDIES
WOMEN WHO KILL ADULTS
SOLITARY KILLERS

Judith Neelley

On September 5th 1982, eighteen year old Judith Neelley, who is described as a sexual predator, stalked, kidnapped, sexually assaulted over three days, tortured, poisoned and murdered thirteen year old Lisa Ann Millican in Rome Georgia.

For three days, Judith sexually abused Lisa Ann, injected her with drain cleaner, shot her and then threw her in the river. Although Judith Neelley had an accomplice, her husband Alvin Howard Neelley, Judith was discovered to be the perpetrator, executor and mastermind behind the sexual assaults and murders. Her husband did provide help with the "heavy lifting" on October 4th 1982 when Judith decided to abduct a young couple Janice Chatman and

John Hancock. Judith and her husband quickly dispatched of the male by shooting him. Judith and her husband kidnapped Janice and brought her back to their hotel room where Judith tortured and murdered her.

For her crimes Judith Neelley is placed at number 22 on Dr. Eli Stone's scale of evil as being a psychopath who inflicts extreme torture on victims before murdering them.

Susan Atkins

Sharon Tate

CASE STUDIES
WOMEN WHO KILL ADULTS
GROUP MURDERS

Susan Atkins

On August 8th 1969 Susan Atkins along with several others known as the "Charles Manson Family" stalked, accosted, induced psychological terror and murder on Sharon Tate. Susan Atkins boasted to a female inmate, while she was imprisoned for a car theft that she alone was responsible for the murder of Sharon Tate, that she had stabbed Tate and tasted her blood. Later on Susan testified in front of a Grand Jury that she had been unable to stab Sharon and blamed the stabbing on another one of her "Manson Family" members. It is alleged that Susan Atkins stabbed Sharon more than sixteen times, tying a rope around her neck to form a crude noose and then attaching that rope to a friend of Sharon's, Jay Sebring. Sharon was nine months pregnant. Susan later stated this was a random murder and that she had not stalked Sharon's house at all, but in the same breath, she states that she and her "Manson Family" indeed drove up and down the streets looking for homes to break into and then to kill the people inside. It is theorized that the death of not only Sharon Tate but the death of all the people in that house that night, was ritual murder, planned with forethought and given insight into the personal lives of the people within. Susan Atkins would be accused of eight murders over the course of her lifespan. At times, she would admit to her involvement, other times she would blame others recanting her stories.

Ultimately for her crimes, Susan Atkins is placed at a number 13, a psychopathic murderer who kills out of rage.

PARANORMAL INFLUENCES

THE DEAMON ABADDON

The Hebrew term *Abaddon* is an intensive form of the word "destruction," and appears as a place of destruction in the Hebrew Bible. In a vision in the Book of Revelation, a male angel called Abaddon is named as the king of an army of locusts, transcribed in Greek as "whose name in Hebrew is Abaddon", "which in Greek means the Destroyer" or Apollyon.

Bill Scott author of The Day Satan Called and radio broadcaster one day while on air received a call from a woman claiming to be part of a witches coven and claiming to be a teenage girl who was about to be sacrificed who was looking for help. Bill describes an eighteen month ordeal where he and his wife, who befriended the girl by taking her home, who turned out to be a thirty year old woman, were plagued by strange happenings in their home and in their lives. Things moving across rooms, lights turning on and off, unseen people jumping on people in the night and hitting them. During the two week period Bill claims the woman spoke in inhuman male voices, the voice of a little girl and voices that had multiple voices within them after which her face would completely contort and change as she would speak these voices.

Bill recounted his story to George Knapp radio broadcaster with Coast to Coast am, that two weeks after he and his wife finally were able to find another place for the woman to live, witnessed a tall dark figure who was clearly standing in the hallway of his home. Bill having been fed up with all the disturbances in his home, blatantly asked the thing, "Tell me why you think you can be in my house?" and Bill says the thing stated to him, as loud as any human voice could be, "I am an invited guest into this home." This absolutely shocked Bill, because not only was he witnessing something he was also being spoken to by it. Bill asked further, "You tell me how!" The thing said, "Have you looked under her bed?" Bill running into the room, where she lived and looking underneath the bed, found occult items belonging to the woman, a poppet doll and some other items. After finding these things he disposed of them as well as the woman's car, which he'd parked in his own driveway. Bill and his wife continued to try and help this woman by attempting to exercise her to no avail. Bill in his selfless attempt to try and help this woman, found a small black book belonging to her whilst searching for items she'd left inside his house, it contained names, addresses and phone numbers. Bill decided to just pick a number and call it, attempting to reach out to anyone who knew the woman. A voice answered, it was the voice of a priest. This is what he said,

"Yes, I know her. Have you spoken to the demon that calls itself Abaddon? Oh, if you had, you'd know it. Once while we were performing an exorcism on her, the entire church began to shake and we could audibly hear something say, "Why do you torture me so?". "I never seen a spirit so strong." After eighteen months of this harrowing ordeal Bill and his wife divorced, the church of the priest he'd spoken to, suffered collapse and disrepair and has become derelict and no one worships there anymore. Bill's friends and people who tried to help the woman also suffered divorce. The woman who had disappeared after Bill and various others had tried to help her suddenly reappeared on the exact day and time that Bill and his wife had decided to separate to announce that she was leaving town. Surely Abaddon, the destroyer had been there and having accomplished its goal, to destroy, it was ready to moved on.

Years later, Bill discovered the woman again, as he was listening to the radio. Again, as if she were re setting the trap, she was on the radio, calling into a station, with the same story, asking for help. Bill hearing this, called the producers at the radio station to relay his harrowing ordeal with this woman, who he had a name for "Susan". Bill was eventually able to track her down at a public park. As Bill approached the picnic table, Susan says, "You found me. Better men than you have tried to cast me out. I'll kill her before I let you have her." Deciding the woman was beyond all help, Bill left that place and has never looked back.

PEOPLE OF THE LIE
THE HOPE FOR HEALING
HUMAN EVIL

SCOTT M. PECK M.D.

Dr. Peck was a psychiatrist and author known for his book, "The Road Less Traveled" published in 1978 and "People of the Lie" published in 1983. In "People of the Lie" Peck describes the stories of several of his patients that were particularly resistant to any form of psychotherapy. He came to think of them as evil and goes on to describe the characteristics of evil in psychological terms. I agree with Dr. Pecks proposition that evil could become a psychiatric diagnosis.

Dr. Peck characterizes evil as a "malignant type of self-righteousness" in which there is an active refusal to tolerate imperfection or guilt.

This syndrome results in a projection of evil onto specific innocent victims (often children). Dr. Peck argues that these people are the most difficult of all to deal with being extremely difficult to classify. ⍰ Some of his conclusions about the psychiatric condition he designates "evil" are derived from his close study of one patient he names Charlene. Although Charlene is not dangerous, she is ultimately unable to have empathy for others in any way.

According to Peck, people like her see others as play things, objects or tools to be manipulated for their uses or to satiate their curiosity. Peck states that these people are rarely seen by psychiatrists and have never been treated successfully.

Evil is also described by Peck as "militant ignorance". Peck argues those that are evil actively and militantly refuse consciousness. Peck considers those he calls evil to be attempting to escape and hide from their own conscience (through self deception) and views this as being quite distinct from the apparent absence of conscience evident in sociopathy.

According to Peck an evil person

Is consistently self deceiving, with the intent of avoiding guilt and maintaining a self image of perfection

Deceives others as a consequence of their own self deception

Projects his or her evils and sins onto very specific targets (scapegoats) while being apparently normal with everyone else ("their insensitivity toward him was selective" (Peck, 1983/1988, p 105[7]))

Commonly hates with the pretense of love, for the purposes of self deception as much as deception of others

Abuses political (emotional) power ("the imposition of one's will upon others by overt or covert coercion" (Peck, 1978/1992, p298[6]))

Maintains a high level of respectability, and lies incessantly in order to do so

Is consistent in his or her sins. Evil persons are characterized not so much by the magnitude of their sins, but by their consistency (of destructiveness)

Is unable to think from the viewpoint of their victim (scapegoat)

Has a covert intolerance to criticism and other forms of narcissistic injury

Most evil people realize the evil deep within themselves but are unable to *tolerate the pain of introspection* or admit to themselves that they are evil. Thus, they constantly run away from their evil by putting themselves in a position of *moral superiority* and putting the focus of evil on others. Evil is an extreme form of what Scott Peck, in *The Road Less Traveled*, calls a **character disorder**.[6][7]

☐Using the My Lai Massacre as a case study Peck also examines group evil, discussing how human group morality is strikingly less than individual morality.[7] Partly he considers this to be a result of specialization, which allows people to avoid individual responsibility and pass the buck, resulting in a reduction of group conscience.

Though the topic of evil has historically been the domain of religion,[7] Peck makes great efforts to keep much of his discussion on a scientific basis, explaining the specific psychological mechanisms by which evil operates. He was also particularly conscious of the danger of a psychology of evil being misused for personal or political ends.[7] Peck considered that such a psychology should be used with great care, as falsely labeling people as evil is one of the very characteristics of evil. He argued that a diagnosis of evil should come from the standpoint of healing and safety for its victims, but also with the possibility even if remote, that the evil themselves may be cured.

Ultimately Peck says that evil arises out of free choice. He describes it thus: Every person stands at a crossroads, with one path leading to God, and the other path leading to the devil. The path of God is the right path, and accepting this path is akin to submission to a higher power. However, if a person wants to convince himself and others that he has free choice, he would rather take a path which cannot be attributed to its being the right path. Thus, he chooses the path of evil.

Peck also discussed the question of the devil.[7] Initially he believed as with '99% of psychiatrists and the majority of clergy' (Peck, 1983/1988,[7] p182) that the devil did not exist but after starting to believe in the reality of human evil, he then began to contemplate the reality of spiritual evil.

Eventually after having been referred several possible cases of possession and being involved in two exorcisms, he was converted to a belief in the existence of Satan. Peck considered people who are possessed as being victims of evil, not evil themselves. Peck however considered possession to be rare, and human evil common. He did believe there was some relationship between Satan and human evil but was unsure of its exact nature. Peck's writings and views on possession and exorcism are to some extent influenced and based on specific accounts by Father Malachi Martin. It is not possible to find formal records to establish the veracity of Fr. Malachi Martin's described cases of possession as all exorcism files are sealed by the Archdiocese of New York, where all but one of the cases took place.

WORKPLACE VIOLENCE RECOGNIZING A FEMALE PREDATOR IN THE WORKPLACE

STALKING

Firstly, it is very common to be stalked in your every day life and the workplace is not immune to stalkers. It is in fact that because we spend most of our lives in the workplace, that you will most likely look for your stalker there as well as in and around your home. This is especially true for girls and single women although married women are very much stalking victims. The female predator as part of her nature, will stalk you, although for most of the duration it goes unnoticed. Stalking presents itself in these ways while in the workplace and this can also be applied to any situation:

Routinely monitors your movements, seems to know where your going, where you've been and what your next few steps are.

Follows you closely and "pops in" or "pops up" allot.

You seem to notice this person a lot, especially during your daily routines, wherein before, you hadn't noticed this person at all so that now their actions closely mirror yours, down to the hours and days.

Suddenly knows your friends and makes an effort to inquire about your contacts, friends and family.

HARASSMENT
PHYSICAL ATTACKS

I have been physically assaulted in the workplace as have so many other people, but when it comes to the female predator the assault takes a variety of shades, neither are any of them grey.

They are cold and concrete evidence, although getting someone to believe you is another in a society that doesn't believe in female predators can be difficult:

Frequent pushes, brushes to the body, knocks or "friendly hits".

Staged accidents or leaving harmful items where they know you will be in contact with them and be potentially hurt.

Gathers others around you via rumor whereby inciting reasons for persons to want to do you harm.

Pretending not to do something that actually ends up hurting you.

SEXUAL ASSAULT

Sexual assault is also very common in the workplace, but how does one factor in the female predator? Look for:

Physical touching that is unwanted but portrayed as being "normal" such as touching ones hair, or body.

Rape via foreign object.

The coercive use of others to assist in the physical touching, rape or other sexual assault such as gathering support for restraint or inciting others to do the harm.

Aggressive touching of the bodies sexual parts or non sexual parts in a sexual manner or manner that gives the perpetrator sexual pleasure.

SABOTAGE
SHAME/DEGREDATION

Often times a female predator will revel in and create opportunities to shame, degrade and sabotage you all for the sick pleasure of doing it, these people do not operate as normal people do having various degrees of evil, which in itself, is a science. Look for:

Manipulation of your behavior in order for her to reach a desired effect either immediate, intermediate or long term.

Points out or makes up in order to bring attention to crude, inappropriate or widely socially unacceptable issues and then surrounds you with them.

Makes statements, or uses actions, subtle or non verbal attacks to your basic human dignity. This can be for professional, political, social or sexual gain.

SELF ASSESSMENT

SURVIVOR, ABUSER, CO-ABUSER

The Survivor: Someone who has had suffered at the hand of a female predator who was either a sibling, mother, aunt, cousin, friend, acquaintance or stranger. The Survivor will have usually sustained injuries over an extended period of time or it may have only been instantaneous.

The Abuser: Someone who has intently injured another, usually over a prolonged period of time. The Abuser is usually someone who is in self denial and thereby denial to others as to the goings on of the abuse. Often times the abuser never acknowledges that any abuse ever took place. This is a person who exerts their will over that of another's regardless of the consequences.

The Co-Abuser: Someone who usually assists in the abuse of the Abuser and will often have the same characteristics of the main abuser.

LONG TERM SILENT WITNESS

The long term silent witness is someone either close to the situation or someone outside of the situation that has a deep knowledge of the abuse but chooses not to tell anyone. Long term silent witnesses can remain silent for years while intimately witnessing abuse as is often the case.

HELP GUIDE

STALKING

Immediately identify the person you believe to be stalking you. Obtain as much information about them as you possibly can. If you don't know the person, friendly engage them in a quick conversation in which you quickly ask their First and Last Name, Address, Phone number and Occupation, try to get an email address. You will need to write this down or memorize it.

Call 911 immediately if you are being followed closely .

File a Police Report. It never hurts to file a report, if something happens, you have an official police record.

Never give out your real name or any identifiers to strangers. In the workplace, it is a very common practice to reveal and celebrate birthdays. This is a violation of personal privacy however widely practiced. You can ask your office manager to remove you from the birthday calendar. In regards to your co workers who will undoubtedly know a lot about you, try to keep as many key things hidden about yourself as possible, especially if someone starts asking about where you live and where you go after work.

Establish a contact log, of every instance the stalker has engaged you, or you've noticed something about the stalker. This could prove very effective evidence if ever your stalker is arrested and you need to provide proof, or you plan to file a restraining order, or police report.

Create a Safety Network by talking about it to everyone you trust, that you think you may have a stalker. The more people you include in your safety network the more secure it can help you feel and be.

For victims of stalking there is an Address Confidentiality Program where the United States Government gives victims (Survivors) a post office box to use in place of their home address, all mail is then forwarded from this box to your home address for more information log onto www.victimsofcrime.org.

Victims of Crime provides stalking victims with the resources, choice options, safety tips, and stalker information designed to assist victims in regaining control over their lives. They also provide helpful information for building successful criminal and civil cases against the stalker, the use of restraining orders, and victims' rights.

ADULT VICTIMS OF CHILD ABUSE

If you are an adult victim of child abuse it is not too late to tell your story. You may find it helpful to first write down your story, to use as a narrative. Its never too late to heal. If you cannot write, then you should speak about it to someone, or tape record your voice as a record. Let no evil go down unashamed in the dark, we must shine a light in the dark places. Punishment is the shining of light on it, even if no formal charges are able to be brought.

VICTIMS IN THE WORKPLACE

If you have experienced an attack in the workplace, fear not you are not alone. If you have been sexually assaulted or battered, verbally assaulted, stalked, shamed, degraded etc…you must bring it to light. Many people do not for fear of losing their employment however, in the United States, for most offenses we are covered by the Equal Employment Opportunity Commission. Although you were attacked by another women, you still need to file a complaint and it will be investigated by the commission. You can do this without fear of being fired because it is a federal offense to fire someone who has filed an EEOC Charge against their employer.

Although, it will be uncomfortable, stand your ground. If you are in a country that does not have such protections for its workers, go to the police and file a report. If there is no such reliable source to report to, you must take extra special precaution to protect yourself. I must say, sometimes you just have to get out of there. If your stalker endangers your life or makes it simply deplorable, it may be prudent to just leave. But saying that to a person who is a "fighter" would simply urge them to stay and "fight it out" but from personal experience, trust me, make a clear assessment, it may include just getting the hell out of there, especially if the situation continues to degrade without any chance of a change. But professional women should always protect themselves by reporting it to an outside government agency, even if the company promises you to rectify the problem. Usually the company will placate you for a period of time until all legal liability has been consumed after which they will swiftly find a reason to let you go, or just fire you outright.

LONG TERM SILENT WITNESS

If you need help with reporting an abuser, here are some things you can do:

Call anonymously to make a report. Write a letter to make a report. Confide in someone you know will make a report.

Get help from a qualified medical professional, anyone, even your emergency room doctor would be willing to help you to disclose what you know as they are "Mandated Reporters". Mandated Reporters are people who are mandated by law to disclose certain behaviors that may put others in danger. Usually these people work in mental health, medical or social services departments.

Don't try to assess yourself as to why you never told anyone. This is a matter for a qualified mental health professional. Trying to give yourself a mental health assessment would be like trying to perform brain surgery on yourself, you just can't do it.

THE ABUSERS

If you realize that you have been in an abusive relationship with someone (s) wherein you were the abuser, or co abuser, it is prudent to tell someone right away. You can simply walk into any police station or hospital emergency room. You can also use the guide given for the Long Term Silent Witness and as well as take the same advice. Don't try to assess yourself, leave it to a qualified mental health professional. What matters is that you and your victims get help as soon as possible.

FOR SINGLE WOMEN & GIRLS

It is important that you talk about this, to people you trust. If you are or have been isolated, the easiest thing to do would be to go into the nearest hospital and ask to speak to a social worker. That social worker will help to guide you towards the help you need.

FOR ISOLATED WOMEN & GIRLS WITHIN FAMILIES

If you are surrounded by people, however, and everyone around you encourages you to make contact with your abuser, then you need to get out of that situation as soon as possible. For many people, this can be a confusing situation as family and friends can be very persuasive and manipulative. You may be in an abusive or dysfunctional family. If you sense that something is wrong or just "not right" about what's happening to you, the easiest thing to do would be to walk into an emergency room and ask to speak to a social worker. This social worker will act as your "cheer leader" representing you and linking you to much needed services. Social Workers can give you an air of credibility in what can sometimes be an unbelieving world. Social Workers can act like protective parents or guardians of the weak and the lost.

FOR GRIEVING FAMILIES & VICTIMS

Its important to talk about what has happened, even in small amounts if even at all. The easiest thing to do would be to create a support group in your neighborhood. Creating a support group helps you feel confident and strong, in the knowledge that you are not alone. A support group is a form of group therapy and helps you to re establish your boundaries. What are Boundaries? Boundaries are the external limits we place around ourselves that make us feel safe and protected. When people push our boundaries or we are made to go outside of our boundaries, we can then feel unsafe and insecure. Abusers are people who literally smash our boundaries to pieces. Abusers show absolutely no regard for our boundaries at all and this is why it is important to always re establish or rebuild your boundaries, when you feel someone has violated them. You can do this by simply and firmly saying, "No." or "No!".

AFTERWORD

Throughout my life, it seems I've come face to face with evil more times than I can count. I know that evil is undoubtedly real, so why all the skepticism? After looking into various red eyed monsters, I have to say, that evil is a science not yet fully understood or widely accepted by the psychiatry community, religious community or society as a whole.

However, I am no Doubting Thomas. I believe, the "thing" exists and I believe that human evil needs to be looked at further with dedicated public and privately funded scientific study. Just like mental illness, I believe that Evil is an epidemic. I believe the perception of evil needs to come out of the aging and decaying closet, that is the minds of the people who disbelieve and enter into the modern age where it has a foothold and is working to destroy the lives of those who believe and those who do not believe in equal measure. So long as we say it doesn't exist, the farther away from understanding evil we will be. And so, evil runs amok until good people shine a light in the dark place.

Lux Perpetua.

J. M. Gordon

J. M. Gordon

ABOUT THE AUTHOR

Jen Gordon is a Writer and independent researcher in the field of behavioral science. She also writes fiction and non fiction novels as well as essays.

She has previously devoted her time to working with the physically and mentally disabled as a Social Worker, particularly those with dual diagnosis mental disabilities and co occurring alcohol and drug abuse problems.

The author hopes this book will give a voice to those who suffer in silence and has a personal commitment to the betterment of all people. She lives in Los Angeles, California.

J. M. Gordon